SpringerBriefs on Case Studies of Sustainable Development

The importance of sustainable development has been realized for at least 60 years, even though the vast majority of people erroneously think this concept originated with the Brundtland Commission report of 1987 on Our Common Future. In spite of at least six decades of existence, we only have some idea as to what is NOT sustainable development rather than what is. SpringerBriefs on Case Studies of Sustainable Development identify outstanding cases of truly successful sustainable development from different parts of the world and analyze enabling environments in depth to understand why they became so successful. The case studies will come from the works of public sector, private sector and/or civil society. These analyses could be used in other parts of the world with appropriate modifications to account for different prevailing conditions, as well as text books in universities for graduate courses on this topic. The series of short monographs focuses on case studies of sustainable development bridging between environmental responsibility, social cohesion, and economic efficiency. Featuring compact volumes of 50 to 125 pages (approx. 20,000—70,000 words), the series covers a wide range of content—from professional to academic—related to sustainable development.

International Poverty Reduction Center In China

Poverty Alleviation Case Analysis In China

Poverty Alleviation Best Practice via Practices and SDG Strategies

Springer

International Poverty Reduction
Center In China
Beijing, China

ISSN 2196-7830 ISSN 2196-7849 (electronic)
SpringerBriefs on Case Studies of Sustainable Development
ISBN 978-981-97-4536-4 ISBN 978-981-97-4537-1 (eBook)
https://doi.org/10.1007/978-981-97-4537-1

This Springer imprint is published by the registered company Springer Nature Singapore Pte Ltd.
The registered company address is: 152 Beach Road, #21-01/04 Gateway East, Singapore 189721, Singapore

Book Editors and Editorial Board

Book Editors: Tan Weiping, Chan Pinghung Joseph
Editor in Chief: Liu Junwen
Deputy Editor in Chief: Li Xin, Jie Ping
Member: Guo Yan, He XiaoLing, Xu Liping, Wang Huixian, Tong Lang, Xu Fei, Yu Hui, Jiang Xin

Acknowledgments

The team would like to express sincere gratitude to the Bill and Melinda Gates Foundation for sponsoring this project and the HKU Beijing Office for providing constant support throughout the project.

The team is grateful to the staff and experts of the University of Hong Kong for their efforts and contribution to this manuscript, led by Dean Hongbin Cai, Jeroen van-den-Berg, Minyi Huang, Jane Gebhart, Ella Lee, Angela Yin, Po Kuen Ho, Kayee Fung, Wenqian Xu, Regan Fung, Jenny Hou, Hongyu Qian, Yunru Cen, Xuan Niu, Jingping Fang, Yinan Cai, Pallavi Jain, Hauyu Wong, Xinghua Shen, Yutong Li, Yucan Gan, Yuming Qiu, Hu Bi, Siman Zhou, Mingjie Ding, Xiaotong Wang, and Eugene Ye.

Contents

Book Description

This case book is a collection of poverty alleviation cases in China, cross-referencing with cases overseas.

Through analysing the different strategies carried out to address the key specific pain-points at the focal regions and villages, via the effort and collaboration of key stakeholders, the book provides an overview of how Sustainable Development Goals (SDGs) by the United Nations could be achieved. While 'No Poverty' is the first goal in the SDGs, the innovative poverty alleviation approaches demonstrated in these cases had tackled more than just one single goal—with solutions towards multiple dimensions of environmental or social issues.

The academic team has carried out further research and analysis based on the solid ground of the International Poverty Reduction Centre in China (IPRCC) cases. The book is structured in two aspects: in the microscopic view, detail of the focal poverty condition and its corresponding solution and impact will be studied; in the macroscopic perspective, it is to identify the insights how the learning could be adopted in other areas with similar condition.

We are very grateful to the IPRCC and Bill & Melinda Gates Foundation for their support to this project.

Evolution from Original Case Reports

The cases are based on the documents from IPRCC. They are well written, informative and have served the reporting purpose on the achievements of the successful poverty alleviation cases of different scenarios in China. These forms the primary data for this case book.

International Poverty Reduction Center In China, *Poverty Alleviation Case Analysis In China*, SpringerBriefs on Case Studies of Sustainable Development,
https://doi.org/10.1007/978-981-97-4537-1_1

Meanwhile, cases have also been selected to form the series of Best Practice to highlight learnings from different key poverty alleviation strategies. The information and data are extracted from Poverty Eradication Awards for Organizational Innovation Pioneers (2018–2020)[1] and Introduction to China Poverty Alleviation Exchange Base.[2]

In order to achieve international alliance on poverty alleviation knowledge sharing, we have been conducting secondary data collection and research to further develop the case—to build on the original descriptive narrative. As such, through the better understanding of the focal issues, areas and organizations—and their respective key challenges and solutions—we have compiled for each case its analysis, comparative studies and relevance of SDGs & ESG (Environmental, Social, Governance) standard. These are all aiming at engaging the readers, leading them to the learning from the cases, and thinking about how to adopt the related SDG strategies. These also serve as the initiatives to facilitate potential cross-region and cross-disciplinary collaboration.

Background: *Poverty Alleviation in China*

China's poverty problem has a long history, and China's poverty alleviation policies are constantly changing with the times. In the last century, Chairman Mao Zedong once pointed out that China's poverty problem was caused by the semi-colonial and semi-feudal system in the past (news.gmw.cn n.d.). After the founding of P.R. China, the old system was overthrown, but the problem of poverty it caused continued to affect the country. However, under the leadership of the Communist Party, China has made significant efforts to address this issue.

China's poverty alleviation process can be roughly divided into five stages. The first stage (1949–1978), small-scale poverty alleviation (news.gmw.cn n.d.). At this stage, Chairman Mao Zedong clearly put forward with "common prosperity" in his report entitled "On the Issue of Agricultural Cooperation" (news.gmw.cn n.d.). The Communist Party of China (CPC) at that point helped the poor by directly providing materials and cash. However, poverty alleviation at this stage only met the basic needs of the poor people temporarily, and this way of poverty alleviation was not sustainable in the long term. In 1978, the number of poor people living in the rural areas, which was about 250 million people, accounted for 25.97% of China's total population and 1/4 of the world's total population living in poverty. (fupin.ednet.cn n.d.).

The second stage (1978–1985) was the stage of system reform to promote poverty alleviation (news.gmw.cn n.d.). The Third Plenary Session of the Eleventh Central Committee of the CPC commenced in 1978, which marked the start of economic system reform. During this period, the reform measures of the rural economic system include the household contract responsibility system, supporting the development of township enterprises. These measures were to turn the People's commune production mode into a capitalist system, which highly stimulated farmers' enthusiasm in agricultural production. Rural economy got promoted and further caused poverty

[1] China State Council Poverty Alleviation and Development Leading Group Office and Editorial Committee of Poverty Alleviation Series Books (Eds., 2020).

[2] International Poverty Reduction Center in China, 2021.

reduction. By 1985, China's rural poor population had reduced from 250 million in 1978 to 125 million with the rural poverty rate down from 30.7% to 14.8%, the average poverty reduction of 17.86 million people per year. In the meantime, framers' net income per capita increased by 2.6 times (Qstheory.cn 2019; fupin.rednet.cn n.d.).

The third stage (1986–2000) was the stage of large-scale development and poverty alleviation (news.gmw.cn n.d.). In June 1986, the State Council of China established the Leading Group for Economic Development in Poor Areas (renamed the Leading Group for Poverty Alleviation and Development of the State Council in 1993), determined the economic development direction across poor provinces, and formed the central government and the province (autonomous region) as two levels of key support (Qstheory.cn 2019; fupin.rednet.cn n.d.). By the end of 1993, the absolute poverty had been reduced to 80 million, an average annual decrease of 6.4 million in the 7 years' period, and the poverty rate dropped to 8.7% (fupin.rednet.cn n.d.). In the same year, the Central Committee of CPC and the State Council promulgated the "National Eight-Seven Poverty Alleviation Plan (1994–2000)", which proposed to "strive to use around seven years to eliminate the rural population in absolute poverty." By the end of 2000, the goals of the "87 Poverty Alleviation Plan" were basically achieved, and the absolute poverty population dropped from 80 million (1993) to 32.09 million. The poverty incidence rate dropped to 3.4%. The basic livelihood of more than 200 million rural poor people had been solved.

The fourth stage (2001–2013) is the stage of poverty alleviation focusing on villages (news.gmw.cn n.d.). At this stage, the poverty alleviation work went deeper into those areas (Qstheory.cn 2019; fupin.rednet.cn n.d.). Based on the fact above, the State Council of China issued the "Outline of China's Rural Poverty Alleviation and Development (2001–2010)" in June 2001, which proposed "to solve the problem of food and clothing for a small number of poor people as soon as possible" (Qstheory.cn 2019). During this period, 148,000 impoverished villages were identified, and poverty alleviation funds, policies and projects were directed to these villages with the aim to improve the villagers' living conditions and raise their income level. Minority areas in the central and western regions of China have become the focus of poverty alleviation and development while the disabled were also included in the scope of support (news.gmw.cn n.d.). At the end of 2012, under the current standard, the rural poor population in China was 98.99 million (news.gmw.cn n.d.). In order to further accelerate the development of poverty-stricken areas, the Central Committee of CPC promulgated and implemented the "Outline for Poverty Alleviation and Development in China's Rural Areas (2011–2020)" in 2011, putting forward with the overall goal: "By 2020, the poor should not worry about food or clothing, and ensure that their compulsory education, basic medical care and housing problems, with the fundamental facilities developed." (fupin.rednet.cn n.d.)

The fifth stage (2013–2021), the stage of targeted poverty alleviation (news.gmw.cn n.d.). General Secretary of CPC Xi Jinping proposed "targeted poverty alleviation" in November 2013 <Decision of the Central Committee of the CPC and the State Council on Winning the Battle of Poverty Alleviation> stated that "In response to the four major issues of "who should help", "who should be helped", "how to help" and "how to retreat", the specific requirements and practical paths for implementing "six precision" and "five batches" are put forward (Qstheory.cn 2019; fupin.rednet.cn n.d.; www.china.com.cn n.d.)." The targeted poverty alleviation strategy has made great achievements in China's poverty alleviation work. The poor population in rural areas had reduced from 98.99 million (2012) to 16.6 million (2018). Over the same period, the poverty rate had reduced to 1.7% (www.china.com.cn n.d.). By 2019, the number of poor people in rural areas had decreased to 5.51 million, and the poverty rate had dropped to only 0.6%. Since 2012, China's rural poor population had reduced by around 10 million people every year. Helen Clark, former administrator of the United Nations Development Program, pointed out: "The scale of China's poverty alleviation has attracted worldwide attention, and the speed is unparalleled!" (www.china.com.cn n.d.)

In 2021 General Secretary Xi declared the success of poverty alleviation in China. To avoid returning to poverty due to various factors, the overall direction and policy for poverty alleviation remained unchanged. As continuity of the rural development, the strategy of rural revitalization which was initiated in 2017 has been introduced to enhance further development across industries.

The above is the brief history of poverty alleviation in China over decades, and it is worth mentioning that in addition to the traditional methods of poverty alleviation, such as improving productivity, China also carried out a series of poverty alleviation strategies with the aim of effectively utilizing local resources and establishing a foundation for further development with collective efforts from stakeholders and collaborative contributors.

References

fupin.rednet.cn. (n.d.). *中国扶贫历史与现状_全国动态_扶贫频道*. [online] Available at: https://fupin.rednet.cn/c/2017/12/11/4499650.htm

news.gmw.cn. (n.d.). *新中国成立以来中国共产党扶贫脱贫事业的演进历程 _光明网*. [online] Available at: https://news.gmw.cn/2020-06/10/content_33899529.htm

Qstheory.cn. (2019). *我国扶贫工作的历程、经验与持续推进的着力点*. [online] Available at: http://www.qstheory.cn/llwx/2019-10/16/c_1125111200.htm

www.china.com.cn. (n.d.). *中国精准扶贫成就彰显世界意义_观点中国_中国网*. [online] Available at: http://www.china.com.cn/opinion2020/2021-01/08/content_77094589.shtml

Overview: The Development

The purpose of this book is to:

- Study the selected cases individually to identify issues that need to be addressed at the individual, village, and agriculture industry levels within their respective social contexts, along with the corresponding concepts and theories.
- Understand the overall landscape collectively by examining the matrix across these different scenarios.
- Inspire potential future initiatives through engagement with local and overseas stakeholders.
- The main structure of the cases involves examining their background, focal organization (or region, institute), key challenges, solutions, case analysis (which includes their relationship with SDG or ESG), comparative overseas cases or best practices in China, and potential future engagement strategies.

Case Selections

Case categories	Case studies	Case studies title (English)
性别平等,提供妇女工作机会	秧洛村平等机会及妇女就业发展	Equal Opportunities and Job Creation for Women at Yangluo Village
教育扶贫	毕节同心农工中等职业技术学校	Bijie Tongxin Agricultural and Industrial Secondary Vocational and Technical School

(continued)

International Poverty Reduction Center In China, *Poverty Alleviation Case Analysis In China*, SpringerBriefs on Case Studies of Sustainable Development,
https://doi.org/10.1007/978-981-97-4537-1_2

(continued)

Case categories	Case studies	Case studies title (English)
文化扶贫	勐根村老达保文化扶贫项目	Cultural and Tourism Development at Menggen Village
旅游扶贫	阿土列尔村“悬崖村”	Atuleer Village ‘The Cliff Village’
孤儿救助	湖南孤儿救助项目	Orphan-Support Program in Hunan Province
激励脱贫	四川省脱贫激励机制	Poverty Alleviation Incentive Scheme in Sichuan Province
利用大数据精准脱贫	定边县大数据菜单式脱贫	Dingbian “Menu-Based” Big Data Poverty Alleviation
发展电商助力脱贫	安徽固镇县农副产品产业与电商融合	Integration of Guzhen Agricultural & Sideline Products with E-Commerce in Guzhen County, Anhui Province
生态移民村	原隆村生态移民	Eco-Migration in Yuanlong Village

Best Practice reference case selections

Cases	Best practice reference cases (Organizations)	Best practice reference cases (Strategies)
Equal Opportunities and Job Creation for Women at Yangluo Village 秧洛村平等机会及妇女就业发展	Huamao Village, Zunyi, Guizhou Province 贵州遵义花茂村	Multi-Disciplinary Poverty Reduction Strategy 综合模式扶贫
Bijie Tongxin Agricultural and Industrial Secondary Vocational and Technical School 毕节同心农工中等职业技术学校	Hainan Poverty Reduction Evening School Television Program Development Task Force Office 海南脱贫致富电视夜校工作推进小组办公室	Poverty Reduction by Education 教育扶贫
Cultural and Tourism Development at Menggen Village 勐根村老达保文化扶贫项目	Qufu, Shandong Province 山东曲阜	Poverty Reduction Through Culture Development 文化扶贫
Atuleer Village “The Cliff Village” 阿土列尔村“悬崖村”	Xiadang Village, Ningde, Fujian Province 福建宁德下党村	Multi-Disciplinary Poverty Reduction Strategy 综合模式扶贫

(continued)

(continued)

Cases	Best practice reference cases (Organizations)	Best practice reference cases (Strategies)
Orphan-Support Program in Hunan Province 湖南孤儿救助项目	Tianjin Women's and Children's Development Foundation 天津妇儿发展基金会	Strengthen Social Assistance to Fight Against Poverty 兜底保障
Poverty Alleviation Incentive Scheme in Sichuan Province 四川省脱贫激励机制	New Folk Style Development Leadership Group Office at Ankang Village in Shanxi Province 陕西安康新民风建设领导小组办公室	Grassroots Governance 基层治理
Dingbian 'Menu-Based' Big Data Poverty Alleviation 定边县大数据菜单式脱贫	Poverty Alleviation and Development Leadership Group Office, Linyi Municipal in Shangdong Province 山东临沂市扶贫开发领导小组办公室	Poverty Alleviation by Financial Aid 金融扶贫
Integration of Agricultural & Sideline Product with E-Commerce in Guzhen County, Anhui Province 安徽固镇县农副产品产业与电商融合	Social Participation in Poverty Alleviation and Development of China 中国社会扶贫网	Povety Alleviation by E-Commerce 电商扶贫
Eco-Migrationin at Yuanlong Village 原隆村生态移民	Hubei Poverty Alleviation Investment and Development Limited Company 湖北扶贫投资开发有限公司	Poverty Alleviation by Relocating the Poor (Plus Supporting Industry and Financial Aid) 易地扶贫(+产业扶贫 + 金融扶贫)

Selected Categories: Key Issues

秧洛村平等机会及妇女就业发展 Equal Opportunities and Job Creation for Women at Yangluo Village	• Lack of investment for housing • Lack of skillsets and capital for agriculture • Lack of economic mobility for domestic and Wa women: Women were usually confined to domestic work and hence had no source of income
毕节同心农工中等职业技术学校 Bijie Tongxin Agricultural and Industrial Secondary Vocational and Technical School	• Low education level of the youth for the development of local industry and economy
勐根村老达保文化扶贫项目 Cultural and Tourism Development at Menggen Village	• Limited source of income (tea) • Transportation infrastructure not sufficient • Low technology mindset
阿土列尔村 "悬崖村" Atuleer Village "The Cliff Village"	• Inconvenient transportation: Lack of infrastructure • Lack of job opportunities • Lack of human resources • Closed management
湖南孤儿救助项目 Orphan-Support Program in Hunan Province	• Orphans who need long term support
四川省脱贫激励机制 Poverty Alleviation Incentive Scheme in Sichuan Province	• Unconditional poverty subsidy cannot inspire the motivation of the impoverished households • A long-term and sustainable solution to poverty reduction is needed
定边县大数据菜单式脱贫 Dingbian Big Data "Menu-Based" Big Data Poverty Alleviation	• Wide range of documents on project execution, creating an information overload for impoverished households; They passively waited for poverty alleviation policies from government officials and were unable to actively choose the most suitable plan for themselves
安徽固镇县农副产品产业与电商融合 Integration of Agricultural & Sideline Product with E-Commerce in Guzhen County, Anhui Province	• Agricultural industry for poverty alleviation faced the issue of limited sales
原隆村生态移民 Eco-Migration in Yuanlong Village	• The complexity in coordination of combined effort of local governmental branch, enterprises and individual villagers with a clear focus on eco-migration

Selected Categories: SDG/ESG—UN's Sustainable Development Goals and Environmental, Social and Governance (ESG) will be combined into the evaluation sector to bring in a more objective and international recognized criteria in assessing the positive impact brought about by the program.

Selected Categories: Key Learnings

秧洛村平等机会及妇女就业发展 Equal Opportunities and Job Creation for Women at Yangluo Village	• Comprehensive Solution to tackle multi-SDGs
毕节同心农工中等职业技术学校 Bijie Tongxin Agricultural and Industrial Secondary Vocational and Technical School	• The school conducted effective talent-cultivation programs; • Evergrande Group provided pairing-off assistance in the poverty alleviation of Dafang county; • The county government organized farmers' training workshops
勐根村老达保文化扶贫项目 Cultural and Tourism Development at Menggen Village	• Cultural Confidence (refer to the white paper "Renlei jianpin de Zhongguo shijian" [人类减贫的中国实践])
阿土列尔村"悬崖村" Atuleer Village "The Cliff Village"	• The balance between the preservation of traditional culture of Yi people and the relocation of villagers (social sustainability); • The economic sustainability of tourism
湖南孤儿救助项目 Orphan-Support Program in Hunan Province	• From vocational education for orphans to help them getting jobs and create income for their whole family: "From giving him fish to teaching him how to fish" (从授之以鱼到授之以渔)

(continued)

(continued)

四川省脱贫激励机制 Poverty Alleviation Incentive Scheme in Sichuan Province	(1) Poverty alleviation initiatives can effectively motivate poor people to seek employment and strengthen their agricultural production capacities; (2) In line with local policies and utilizing available local resources in order to be effectively implemented
定边县大数据菜单式脱贫 Dingbian Big Data "Menu-Based" Big Data Poverty Alleviation	• How to allocate the major industries reasonably and efficiently at vast area is major consideration;
安徽固镇县农副产品产业与电商融合 Integration of Agricultural & Sideline Product with E-Commerce in Guzhen County, Anhui Province	1. Access and connections between village supply and city demand; 2. Imrprove business plan and pricing model; 3. Reduce logistics costs; 4. Increase supports from experienced urban workforce; 5. Transfers property ownership to be fully controlled by farmers; and 6. Increase volume, size, and quality of the business model to more villages
原隆村生态移民 Eco-Migration in Yuanlong Village	• Coordinated primary, secondary and tertiary industries; • Combined efforts of the local governmental branch, enterprises and individual villagers

Equal Opportunities and Job Creation for Women at Yangluo Village

For sustainable economic development, men's and women's contributions to society as individuals, workers, and citizens are vital. Often, women face various barriers to achieve financial stability because of limited access to economic resources and the lack of roles in decision-making despite being at the frontline of fighting against poverty on household and community levels. At the same time, men also have limited participation in household management and the care of children and elderly within the family unit. As a result, the exclusion of either men or women from making economic and social contributions leads to exploitation, inequalities, and unsustainable development. Therefore, interventions, whether grassroots or government-led, have a levelling effect that engages both genders in productive activities that facilitate economic development by breaking down the traditional gender roles hindering disadvantaged groups (SDC & DFA 2003).

In this case, we will explore the developmental implementation to reduce gender and ethnic barriers in achieving financial autonomy at a village with predominantly *Wa* (佤) population. Villages similar to Yangluo can be found across the Eastern China, often with one major ethnic minority group. The *Wa* people are among the 55 officially recognized ethnic minorities in China; they have around 431,000 people (National Bureau of Statistics of China 2021). The Yangluo village poverty alleviation case can be seen as a success story in realizing how poverty alleviation is affected by the intersectionality of ethnicity and gender.

Gender Equality for Indigenous Women in Rural China

For historical reasons, including barriers to migration, the spatial distribution of poverty of China's minority ethnic population differs from that of the majority Han population (Gustafsson and Sai 2009). In 2017, 53.6% of the rural poor population

International Poverty Reduction Center In China, *Poverty Alleviation Case Analysis In China*, SpringerBriefs on Case Studies of Sustainable Development,
https://doi.org/10.1007/978-981-97-4537-1_3

was concentrated in western China, with a total of 16.3 million. Minorities were more likely to fall into poverty due to their disadvantageous geographic location. The minorities in China's Western provinces such as Yunnan, Guizhou, Gansu, Tibet, and Xinjian tend to have lower household income comparing with those from other regions of China (Gustafsson and Sai 2009). Certain places of these provinces were designated as the pilot area to test the effectiveness of poverty policies which are catered to the unique characteristics of the region.

The phenomenon of indigenous women facing disproportionate difficulties in escaping extreme poverty can be seen globally. Indigenous women have long had a role as protectors and preservers of cultural values and heritage, and like many other women, they are the main caretakers of the family. However, most indigenous women are often unable to create economic opportunities for themselves because of their illiteracy and lack of mobility. They are confined to domestic activities because of traditions within their ethnic groups. The *hukou* policy in China (household registration system 户籍制度) has also made migration out of the countryside difficult and divided citizens broadly between urban and rural subsystems (Chan 2021). Hence, not many ethnic minorities migrated to Tier 1 and 2 cities such as Shanghai, Guangzhou, and Shenzhen to develop their career.

Yangluo Village: Poverty, Ethnic Minorities, and Geography in Yunnan

Yangluo village is an ecological village that strongly preserves its *Wa* culture. Located 10 km to the east of Ximeng County, there are 15 villager groups with 706 households and 2,386 people, including 333 households registered as poverty-stricken. In around 2016, when targeted poverty alleviation was fully implemented, the incidence of poverty was 47%, accounting for nearly half of the households in this village. Yangluo village presents a special case in which its poverty alleviation project targeted women specifically when creating economic opportunities because of the barriers created by historical gender roles within the Indigenous *Wa* group.

The Key Challenges

Due to the systemic poverty and the need for new capital investment to revitalize the local economy, Ximeng County used a top-down approach to alleviate poverty within the female demographic by creating specific job opportunities that allow them to work from home.

Yangluo village took the initiative in poverty alleviation by leveraging government housing subsidies and capital from the village and related companies. It provided (a) safe and secure housing, then (b) created job opportunities for the local people by the agricultural companies, and finally (c) created women's economic initiatives with vocational training. This case study specifically explores the women's initiatives implemented in Yangluo village to understand the specific catalysts required to lift Indigenous *Wa* women out of poverty.

For Yangluo village, understanding how to mobilize the women in the workforce to prevent them from falling into poverty was key when implementing policies to alleviate poverty. On a local level, most residents were able to achieve a higher income level after investment into 16 industrial poverty alleviation projects, totally CNY 12.23 million, which was facilitated by the "four full coverage" method of promotion, interest, connection, and technical training.

Another main implementation was the revitalization of the four pillar industries, sugarcane production, tea-picking, livestock-raising, and beekeeping.

Sugarcane Industry

In the sugarcane industry, the model of "enterprise + village collective + farmer" was adopted; Meng Lian Changyu Sugar Industry Co., Ltd. (孟连昌裕糖业有限责任公司), signed a sugarcane purchase agreement with farmers to plant 1,960 *mu* (亩, a Chinese measuring unit, equivalent to 666.67 m^2) of sugarcane. The annual output is 6,860 tons, which helped 160 households to increase their income by more than CNY 15,000 per household.

Tea Industry

In the tea industry, the model of "production base + agricultural cooperative + farmers" was adopted. Tea factories (cooperatives) provide agri-products such as fertilizer and purchase fresh leaves from farmers. This in turn enable farmers to have a steady income. The local tea industry plants 1,200 mu of tea, with an annual output value of CNY 800,000, employing 175 laborers. The average household income increased by more than CNY 4,000.

Livestock Industry

In the livestock industry, CNY 1.283 million was invested to build four breeding bases for pigs and piglets, by adopting the model of "large capable households + poor households." 626 people from 200 poor households were provided with three piglets from larger breeding households. The value of the pigs increases by CNY 600 each year, for CNY 1,800 in total additional income.

Beekeeping Industry

In the beekeeping industry, through the "enterprise + village collective + poor households" model, local government purchased bee for the poor households to start their business and provided beekeeping training to them. Order purchases were made through an agreement with Yunnan Dingshi Bee Industry and Trade Co., Ltd. (云南丁氏蜂业工贸有限公司).

However, at the local level, there are differences between the male and female population. Women may find it harder to take advantage of the job opportunities from agriculture such as beekeeping, cattle-raising, and tea-picking if they have to do domestic activities such as caring for children. As a result, women have (a) limited mobility and (b) limited capital, which are the key challenges in escaping poverty. These prevent female people from stabilizing their income and approaching gender equality.

Solutions

To address the challenges faced by *Wa* women, Yangluo village implemented a specific policy centered around them. Following the "company + production base + women + intangible heritage" model, the local government established the *Wa* brocade-weaving women's poverty alleviation workshop base by collaborating with Ximeng Impression Ethnic Culture Co., Ltd. (西盟印象民族文化有限公司), a company dedicated to training women with labor records, left-behind women, disabled women, and those willing to participate in the training It aligned with the goal and task of Ximeng County to uplift poverty-stricken villages (Pu'er Shi 2019).

As part of this initiative, Jiangsan Muluo Vocational Training School (江三木落职业培训学校) and the "Beautiful Village: Women's Academy" (美丽乡村:女子学堂) were established in Yangluo Village. These institutions aimed to teach *Wa* women the art of brocade weaving skills and nurture their vocational potential.

Through these efforts, the poverty alleviation workshop base successfully trained over 3,000 indigenous *Wa* women in weaving, significantly contributing to poverty alleviation. As a result, more than 2,000 women have acquired expertise in handloom weaving.

Results

Yangluo village is only one of the many successful stories of rural poverty alleviation. Below are the key indicators of their results in 2019. The key to their success lies in the model, which incorporates intangible heritage and a sustainable business model which provides steady income to *Wa* women and helps them out of poverty. As an intangible cultural heritage, the extraordinary *Wa* brocade is uniquely competitive in marketing. The product brought an average annual income of over CNY 6,400 per person to rural women in 2019 and will continue to provide future income. The specialty item has successfully led weaver producers out of poverty in the long term by establishing the industry. In 2019, the per capita disposable income of Indigenous residents in Yangluo village was CNY 8,640. Hence, *Wa* women fulfilled their wish to "work at home and earn money at home," and they can balance their economic development and family responsibilities.

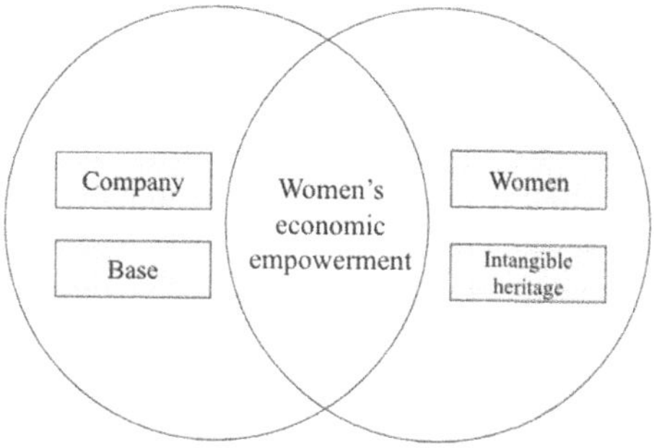

Key Indicators of Results of Poverty Alleviation:

Dimension	Results
Women's income equality	Average annual income of more than CNY 6,400 per person
Women's housing security	All 706 households in Yangluo village have secure and stable housing
Women's employment opportunities	Four *Wa* Brocade Women's Poverty Alleviation workshop bases established with more than 3,000 women trained
Women's poverty mentality	*Wa* women were able to become independent, empowered, and materially self-sufficient, ridding themselves of their poverty mentality

Case Analysis

Development-Centred Poverty Relief Policies

From the government's viewpoint, the development of industries is regarded as the most effective and sustainable way to eliminate poverty in rural areas.

China has fully considered its actual conditions, and launched a series of guidelines and measures to increase efficiency of poverty alleviation, summarized as "Targeted Efforts in Six Areas" and "Five Measures for Poverty Alleviation":

The "Targeted Efforts in Six Areas" refer to:

1. to identify the poor accurately;
2. to arrange targeted programs;
3. to utilize capital efficiently;
4. to take household-based measures;
5. to dispatch first Party secretaries based on village conditions; and
6. to achieve the set goals.

The "Five Measures for Poverty Alleviation" refer to:

- to boost the economy to provide more job opportunities;
- to relocate poor people from inhospitable areas;
- to compensate for economic losses associated with reducing ecological damage;
- to improve education in impoverished areas; and
- to provide subsistence allowances for those unable to shake off poverty through their own efforts alone.

Yangluo village adopted a productivity development approach to eliminate poverty. It is also a long-term plan to increase local employment opportunities, which brings long-term job stability for local peasants. This is achieved with governmental support, which guides poor areas to develop special industries case by case according to local conditions.

From a broader societal perspective, rallying the local community can lead to rapid and effective poverty alleviation in rural areas. Poverty alleviation and reduction is a difficult and complex systemic project that requires the active participation of all parties. The Chinese government extensively and effectively mobilized and pooled the efforts of all parties, including the government itself, the society, and the market, to build a specialized and sectoral poverty alleviation system for specific needs in corresponding locations. The social poverty alleviation system in China is supported by cross-departmental, cross-unit, and community-wide participation to foster talents, capitals, and technology in poor areas. Also, entities with strong market development ability are mobilized to enter areas with high potential for resource development to achieve complementary advantages, mutual benefits, and common development. Regional disparities can be narrowed in this process.

Poverty alleviation in Chinese villages is not centered on relief but on development. By exploring the potentials of the people and the region, adjusting policies according to local conditions, and making precise poverty alleviation guidance, poverty from the root cause of unfavorable geography and economic conditions is eliminated.

Material and Psychological Effects of Establishing Women's Training Centers

On material level, providing Indigenous women with skills training suitable to their situations can encourage female employments. In this circumstance, gender equality is promoted. As mentioned above, the Indigenous women faced the difficulties of limited mobility that men did not face, making them more difficult to take advantage of employment opportunities created by agriculture.

These challenges are not limited to Yangluo village. According to the "Outline for the Development of Chinese Women," from 2011 to 2020, China trained 10.21 million impoverished women with various skills. As a result, more than 5 million impoverished women increased their income and escaped poverty through employments in the fields of handicrafts, farming, learning home economics, and employing e-commerce.

On psychological level, by tapping into rural women's productive potential and stimulating their internal drive, the women are more self-sufficient in the long term and become empowered spiritually. Due to differences in physical capabilities, in traditional rural families, men do the farming work and women take care of the family. Women might be used to being financially dependent on their spouses.

According to Xi Jinping's "Excerpts from Poverty Alleviation," "poverty alleviation is not only about enriching people's pockets but also their minds." The development of poor areas can only depend on people's endogenous motivation for a sustainable income. Instead of directly giving subsidies to the villages, the government tends to use investment for development of local industries. In alleviating poverty, women's economic development and ideological construction are carried out synchronously. Rural women's poverty alleviation is achieved by improving their basic skills of production and business, which increases their potential and contributes to positive psychological incentives.

In addition, establishing a mechanism for learning from each other is also effective in motivating poor women to rely on work to create happiness. Their mind-set can be changed by the virtuous circle of positive psychological incentives. The concept of "preferring hard work to hard wait" might be deeply rooted psychologically in women. When helping women get out of poverty, it is also important to alter their mentality in terms of their awareness and thinking about poverty.

Additionally, "the red and black list" (红黑榜), i.e., lists of positive behavior on red list and lists of negative behavior on blacklist, was updated once a week in the village to inform everyone who the good and bad performers in various work are, can competitively motivate the women's career spirit in brocade weaving, and cultivate their self-reliance and psychological power.

Thus, skills training increases rural women's employment opportunities, gives women the freedom to own economic resources, along with promoting equity of opportunity and wealth. It also stimulates women's potential, increases internal drive, empowers women mentally, and promotes rural gender equality.

Best Practice

Development is the principle for solving all of China's problems, including the problem of poverty mentioned by Xi. China's poverty reduction practice shows that development is the most effective way to eliminate poverty and the most stable way to lead a happy life. Only through development can the basic rights of all people, including women, be better protected; only then can people's desire for a better life be continuously met.

Best Practice Case: Huamao Village, Zunyi, Guizhou Province—Multi-disciplinary Poverty Reduction Strategy

Huamao Village, located in the remote and mountainous region of Guizhou Province, was previously plagued by poverty due to the historical underdevelopment of the province—Guizhou Province was one of the least developed provinces in China. In the past, the village encountered significant challenges as nearly half of its population had migrated to urban areas in pursuit of better-paid jobs. Out of the original 4,000 villagers, approximately 2,000 had departed, leaving behind mostly elderly residents and children, thus categorizing Huamao as a "left-behind" village.

Through initiatives such as the promotion of cultural rural tourism, the development of efficient modern agriculture, the revitalization of local crafts, and the reconstruction of infrastructure within the village, Huamao has successfully transformed itself into a thriving community and an appealing destination for visitors.

Huamao Village is known for its 400-year-old ceramic industry, which produces clay pottery ware used as containers for Maotai (茅台), a famous brand of Chinese liquor. For example, Mu Xiancai, a 52-year-old potter, founded his first workshop in Huamao as the local government began to boost rural tourism in 2014. Mu's family has been making clay pottery for generations, which is now an intangible part of the village's cultural heritage.

Mu's workshop soon became a popular tourist destination as he expanded his pottery shop into a farm stay by integrating the pottery-making experience, education, catering, and residence. People can purchase pottery artwork and experience the fun of making ceramics themselves.

Papermaking and ceramic crafts are symbols of Huamao, and these could strengthen the cultural identity of the village by raising its profile, boosting tourism, and lifting people out of poverty.

Making paper by boiling the bark of mulberry trees is an old tradition in the village. Shengdi Zhang (张胜迪), founder of a papermaking workshop called Huamao Renjia (花茂人家), i.e., literally "households of Huamao," who left the village for better job before, returned to Huamao and started the workshop by using the ancient method. Zhang said she believes the root cause of poverty lies in the lack of culture, and she hopes to revive the traditional craft as part of the effort to reduce poverty (Su et al. 2023).

Twelve local villagers are now working in Zhang's workshop, which receives more than half a million tourists every year. As cultural tourism prospers, more migrant workers are returning to Huamao. For Zhang, her dream of helping Huamao end poverty through reviving traditional culture is more likely to come true.

The beautification initiatives undertaken in Huamao have also contributes to cultural tourism and people's livelihood. The transformation of housing with ethnic features, the installation of solar-powered streetlights, and the planting of trees have enhanced the aesthetics of the village while also promoting sustainability.

With the improved environment, Huamao began to receive an increasing number of tourists who are seeking an authentic rural experience in 42 homestays and 10 agriculture-experiencing farm stays. These improvements have led to a significant increase in the number of tourists, with Huamao now welcoming 1.5 million annually compared to around 100,000 tourists in the past.

Rural cooperatives also allowed villagers who remained as farmers to develop their paths in local tourism or craftsmanship. However, despite those who prospered by developing rural tourism or traditional craftsmanship, a number of villagers relied on agriculture for a living. The village thus established rural cooperatives which turned various smaller agricultural businesses into a large-scale collective industry.

At present, the annual income of local villagers has exceeded CNY 17,000, an increase of over 30% compared to that of 2014. And 78 households that were registered as being under the poverty line in 2014 have all been lifted out of poverty.

"Currently, there are only about 300 villagers working outside the Guizhou Province," The First Secretary of the village, Pan said, regarding the big changes in the village, 'many migrant workers chose to come back because they can now either start their own business or find a decent job in Huamao.'

A construction and infrastructure upgrade has achieved wealth, knowledge, happiness, and beauty in this rural area. Their five initiatives were coordinated industries development, rural civilization, clean and sustainable villages, positive governance effects, and continuous livelihood and well-being improvement.

International Comparative Studies

The Yangluo village model of equal opportunities has universal applications which could also be applied in other countries of similar barriers to developing women's equality.

South Africa: Liberating Rural Women Through Skills Training for Poverty Alleviation

Women comprise rural South Africa's largest population, but few have formal education or training. To alleviate their poverty, the Department of Higher Education and Training instituted community education through Community Colleges for the underprivileged, prioritizing women in order to empower them with life skills for self or industrial employment.

However, despite these efforts, most women remain unskilled and, consequently, unemployed, which have deepened their poverty situaion. The training programs include Early Childhood Development, Community Development Works Programmes, Worker Education, Plumbing, Construction, Carpentry, Electricity, Welding, and Auto Body Repairs to empower rural women and reduce poverty. However, most of these skills are of no use to women or do not help with their livelihoods' improvement. Instead, women in the study responded that they would rather engage in courses which can empower them with livelihood skills such as basket weaving, arts and crafts, fashion design, catering, and others.

This upskilling strategy draws parallels with the *Wa* brocade-weaving skills training center in Yangluo village, which turned out to be successful because it did not require additional literacy skills and concerned the villagers' own cultural heritage. Hence, establishing a concentrated, skill training center such as that of Yangluo village, like basket-weaving, could potentially provide better outcomes to women from rural South African in income generation. In addition, self-employment could also increase if the local government adopted a poverty alleviation model which is similar to Yangluo village's "company + base + women + heritage" model This model helps kickstart entrepreneurial endeavors by working with a company to generate consistent demand.

Peru: Empowering Women in Rural Domestic Settings

In rural Peru, women also found themselves in perpetual poverty because of the traditional patriarchal culture. Men's work was more valued than women's because of their physical strength, despite women also do labour-intensive jobs such as cattle-raising, milking, and even harvesting crops. In addition, men often left the communities to work in urban areas or mines, leaving the women to stay at home as the primary caretaker, and take on the labour-intensive roles of men. It was understood that the lack of funding for women because of their lack of assets and capital, while men own everything, including land and animals.

Adopting the model from Yangluo village's "company + base + women + intangible heritage" could potentially allow women in Peru to develop their skills and start their own small businesses. In this model, initial capital was provided by the local governments, which is similar to the case of Yangluo where local government invested in a training center, while the Chinese government subsidized the locals' housing renovations. This would allow women to alleviate poverty by enabling them to work at home. In addition, the traditional, oppressive patriarchal structure could potentially improve as women gained a larger representation in their local community. This will help to consolidate their decision-making position.

India: Upskilling Female Rural-to-Urban Migrant Workers

In 2019, four vocational training centers were established in the rural state of Karnataka, India. The centers provided vocational skills and a guaranteed employment match in urban Bangalore following training for more than 1,000 women. However, COVID-19 pandemic disrupted operations of these centers, and adversely affected the effectiveness of the vocational training centers.

As a result, the initial uptake of vocational training was low. Overall, among households with eligible women in 12 villages, the participation rate at the four vocational training centers was 8.2%. Most participants were unmarried and 18–35 years old, with relatively high mobility. Most of these women also faced fewer competing demands for their time, such as not needing to fetch water that can be a burdensome and time-consuming task in rural areas, allowing them to allocate more time and energy to participate in vocational training or other activities. Rather than rural-to-urban migration, there was reverse migration from urban to rural areas, and this has affected the economic prospects of the women.

Because Yangluo village did not expect rural women to migrate to urban areas, their weaving training could be done in their own village, and at their own homes. By working with a company which generated demand for their products, rural women did not need to migrate to urban areas, where living costs were higher. This has potentially increased the severity of their poverty. They were able to earn a decent income by working in their home villages. This model potentially reduced the issues seen in the upskilling program for rural female workers.

Sustainable Development Goals and Key Learning Objectives

The Department of Economic and Social Affairs of the United Nations provided a shared blueprint for peace and prosperity for all people and the planet, now and into the future. At its heart are the 17 Sustainable Development Goals (SDGs): No poverty; Zero hunger; Good health and well-being; Quality education; Gender equality; Clean water and sanitation; Affordable and clean energy; Decent work and economic growth; Industry, innovation, and infrastructure; Reduced inequalities; Sustainable cities and communities; Responsible consumption and production;

Climate action; Life below water; Life on land; Peace, justice, and strong institutions; Partnerships for the goals. The following goals are achieved in this case.

SDG 1: No Poverty

This goal refers to ending poverty in all its forms everywhere. The main purpose of this goal is to build resilience of the poor and those in vulnerable situations and reduce their exposure and vulnerability to climate-related extreme events and other economic, social, and environmental shocks and disasters. Then, this goal also tends to ensure that all men and women, in particular, the poor and the vulnerable, have equal rights to economic resources in a variety of ways. This would include enhanced development cooperation and creating sound policy frameworks at the national, regional, and international levels, based on pro-poor and gender-sensitive development strategies, to support accelerated investment in poverty eradication. In this case, through the above-mentioned resources and women-friendly industrial design, the women's industry of Wa brocade weaving in Yangluo village was developed, and rural women who learned to weave can continuously bring profits to the village. According to the State Council of China, the Central government decided to set the per capita net income of farmers at CNY 2,300 as the national poverty line, while the average annual income of each female brocade weaver reached over CNY 6,400 in 2019, which creates a sustainable and persistent exit from poverty.

SDG 5: Gender Equality

This goal refers to the achievement of gender equality and the empowerment of all women and girls.

This means ensuring women's full and effective participation and equal opportunities for leadership at all levels of decision-making in political, economic, and public life. In this case, in the past, rural women, because of limited mobility and capital constraint, tended to take the responsibility of taking care of their families and they were unable to obtain suitable work opportunities, and relying only on the economic resources brought by men's work. Under the policy in Yangluo village, women can engage in Wa brocade-weaving production and have similar sufficient work opportunities and vocational training opportunities as men. Additionally, they also receive payment similar to that of men. (In 2019, the average annual income of each woman weaver was over CNY 6,400. This was close to the per capita disposable income of CNY 8,640 for rural residents in Yangluo Village.) Clearly, creating employment opportunities for women can promote gender equality in the economic field.

SDG 8: Decent Work and Economic Growth

This goal refers to promoting sustainable and inclusive economic growth, full and productive employment, and decent work for all. This means promoting development-oriented policies which support productive activities, decent job creation, entrepreneurship, creativity, and innovation, and encourage the formalization and growth of micro-, small- and medium-sized enterprises. Besides, achieving full and productive employment and decent work for all women and men includes disabled people, and equal pay for work of equal value. In this case, skills training (e.g., Jiangsan Muluo Vocational Training School) develops the potential productivity of rural women and arranges suitable jobs which meet the needs of rural women. For instance, rural women cannot work far from home because they are taking care of children. *Wa* brocade-weaving enables women to work at home and earn money at home, a job which meets the special needs of rural women and promotes their full employment.

SDG 10: Reduced Inequalities

The goal refers to reducing inequality within and among countries. This means adopting policies, especially fiscal, wage, and social protection policies, and progressively achieving greater equality. Also, official development assistance and financial flows are encouraged, including foreign direct investment, for area in much need of support. In this case, Yangluo village uses the financial poverty alleviation policy to bring companies from more developed areas outside the village into the less developed village (introduction of "Ximeng Impression"), to provide sales channel for village women to sell their handmade products. At the same time, the establishment of the assistance base (Jiangsan Muluo Vocational Training School) promotes the development of Yangluo village, and reduce the gap between the backward areas and developed areas in China. Then, regional inequality is reduced.

In conclusion, the "company + base + women + intangible heritage" model can help alleviate the poverty of disadvantaged women, where regional circumstances fit. Development-centered poverty relief policies such as vocational training centers have been proven effective in alleviating poverty in rural China.

References

Briefing. (n.d.). Huamao Village 花茂村. In *Quanguo tuopin gongjian jiaoliu jidi jianjie (xie ce) 全国脱贫攻坚交流基地简介 (下册)* [Introduction to the National Exchange Base for Poverty Alleviation (Volume 2)] (pp. 186–191).

Chan, K. W. (2021, November). *Internal migration in China: Integrating migration with urbanization policies and hukou reform.* Global Knowledge Partnership on Migration and Development

(KNOMAD). https://www.knomad.org/sites/default/files/2022-01/Policy%20Brief%2016-%20Internal%20Migration%20in%20China-Integrating%20Migration%20with%20Urbanization%20Policies%20and%20Hukou%20Reform-Nov%2021.pdf

Gustafsson, B., & Sai, D. (2009). Temporary and persistent poverty among ethnic minorities and the majority in rural China. *Review of Income and Wealth, 55*(s1), 588–606. https://doi.org/10.1111/j.1475-4991.2009.00332.x

National Bureau of Statistics of China. (2021). *China statistical yearbook*. China Statistics Press. Retrieved November 15, 2021, from http://www.stats.gov.cn/sj/ndsj/2021/indexeh.htm

Pu'er Shi Dianzi Shangwu Gonggong Fuwu Xinxi Hua Pingtai. (2019) *Ximeng yinxiang minzu wenhua youxian gongsi 西盟印象民族文化有限公司* [Ximeng Impression Ethnic Culture Co., Ltd]. https://www.pedzsw.com/ppjsInfo/150/40

Su, Y., Tu, M., Peng, Y., Zhang, R., & Xu, X. (2023, February 13). Nostalgia and vitality merge in small village in SW China's Guizhou. *People's Daily*. http://en.people.cn/n3/2023/0213/c90000-10206737.html

Swiss Agency for Development and Cooperation (SDC), & Federal Department of Foreign Affairs (DFA). (2003). *Gender equality: A key for poverty alleviation and sustainable development*. https://www.oecd.org/dac/gender-development/SDC_Gender%20Policy.pdf

Bijie Tongxin Agricultural and Industrial Secondary Vocational and Technical School

Education is the most powerful weapon which you can use to change the world
—*Nelson Mandela* (Mandela 1990)

With the largest and most widely distributed impoverished population, Guizhou Province in southwest China was a key battlefield in poverty alleviation. In addition to the extreme living environment and the lack of infrastructure, the low education level was a decisive factor in intergenerational transmission of poverty. Recent research conducted by UNESCO (UN Educational, Scientific, and Cultural Organization) reveals a strong correlation between poverty and the accessibility of education. It is estimated that if every adult can be provided with two more years of education, 60 million people can be lifted out of poverty (UNAA 2017).

Neglecting children's education was ubiquitous among the villagers in Dafang County, resulting in a high dropout rate. According to the figures published by the provincial government, only 78.6% of school-aged children in Guizhou were enrolled in compulsory education in 2012, while the national average was significantly higher at 91.8% (Li and Yang 2020). Moreover, the schools in rural areas could not provide high-quality educational resources and career orientation for students. In such an educational environment, youth cannot avoid the poverty they inherit from their parents due to the lack of professional knowledge and skills (State Council Information Office 2021). These challenges made poverty alleviation an arduous mission to the Guizhou provincial government.

One of the first targeted poverty educational alleviation projects carried out in Guizhou, Bijie Tongxin Agricultural and Industrial Secondary Vocational and Technical School (Tongxin School), opened in 2010. Since its establishment, the school has been continuously inspected by government officials for further improvements to meet students' lifelong study needs and combine academic achievements with real production output. Despite numerous difficulties, including limited teaching

International Poverty Reduction Center In China, *Poverty Alleviation Case Analysis In China*, SpringerBriefs on Case Studies of Sustainable Development,
https://doi.org/10.1007/978-981-97-4537-1_4

resources, Tongxin School has achieved tremendous success over the past decade as an experiment of poverty alleviation project through education.

To overcome the sustainable development challenges that nations face and meet the poverty reduction target, it is crucial to cultivate more people of high-quality education. This case study aims to demonstrate the remarkable contribution of Tongxin School in poverty alleviation and help to facilitate opinion exchanges and future implementation of similar projects on a global scale. To reflect the effectiveness of this project in a more objective and comprehensive way, the following sections will introduce sustainable development goals (SDGs) and environmental, social, and governance (ESG) factors as evaluation criteria.

Key issues to be addressed in this case study are:

1. poverty alleviation through the establishment of educational institutions in China;
2. the measures taken to tackle poverty through improving education; and
3. the experiences provided by the success of Tongxin School program.

China's Efforts in Poverty Alleviation

In 2015 in Guizhou Province, Chinese President Xi Jingpin addressed the alleviation of poverty and the need to build a moderately prosperous society as a common responsibility of both the nation and the CPC. China is by far the largest developing country in the world, and its relatively weak foundation in terms of infrastructure, education, and sanitation pose challenges to the Chinese government to initiate effective measures to reduce poverty. The Chinese government has set out to conquer these difficulties step-by-step with a range of targeted poverty alleviation policies. At a gathering in February 2022, General Secretary Xi of the CPC declared solemnly: "Victory in the battle against poverty has been achieved. China has completed the arduous task of eliminating extreme poverty" (State Council Information Office 2021).

The national policies enacted by the CPC displayed a transition from individual measures tested in a village to a nationwide comprehensive strategy. From the "Seventh Five-Year Plan" in 1986 to now, the policy toolbox of the government has become more diversified and targeted throughout decades. The national policies covered a variety of areas, incorporating the sectors of culture, science and technology, health, and education, and a brand-new criteria of policy evaluation was created in 2017 to evaluate the effectiveness of the national policies, which was the poverty exit mechanism.

From its international experience, the Chinese government has summarized the guideline of poverty reduction as "Targeted Efforts in Six Areas[1]" and "Five Measures

[1] Six Areas: Identify the poor accurately, arrange targeted programs, utilize capital efficiently, take household-based measures, dispatch first Party secretaries based on village conditions, and achieve the set goals.

for Poverty Eradication.[2]" These guiding principles helped the government to identify those truly in need and devise targeted policies. Among the five batches of targeted measures for different groups, improving education focuses on the root cause of rural impoverishment. To lighten the burden of impoverished families, since 2001, the Chinese government has implemented a "two exemptions and one subsidy (两免一补)" policy to exempt miscellaneous expenses and book fees, as well as subsidize the accommodation fee for impoverished students from rural areas. Until 2007, over 50 million students benefited from this policy ("Liangmian Yibu" 2022). In 2017, the "12-year compulsory education" policy was first introduced, and has gradually been implemented across the country, starting in areas with dense ethnic minorities and developed coastal areas ("Shi'er Nian Yiwu Jiaoyu" 2022).

The Chinese government has continuously offered support to schools in rural areas and extended compulsory education to all the school-age children in order to prevent poverty from being passed down to the next generation. Key institutions of higher education have admitted over 700,000 students from poor villages designated by the state. These measures opened channels for the youth from disadvantaged families to change their fate through education.

Guizhou Province and Its Key Challenges

With the wide distribution of its large impoverished population, Guizhou Province has long been the focus of China's poverty alleviation. In 2021, around 4.39 million impoverished people in Guizhou lived in remote and barren mountain areas (Guiyang Poverty Alleviation Office 2021, p. 16). In addition to its backward natural conditions and insufficient basic infrastructure, several anthropic difficulties were also encountered by Dafang County in Bijie city, Guizhou Province. These challenges mainly included widely distributed ethnic minorities, universal neglect of education, and the problems of children left behind.

First, a wide range of culture and languages flourishes in Guizhou Province, as the home of ethnic minorities, but the diversity of ethnicities also leads to difficulties in communication. Up to 33.2% of Dafang county's population are ethnic minorities, which includes Bai, Yi, Miao, Dai, and Hui minorities ("The Viewport of Dafang" 2022). Many jobs require fluent Mandarin as a prerequisite, which most of the local population do not speak. Coupled with teachers' salaries frequently being in arrears, the long-standing inadequacy of teachers in Guizhou proved to be a major challenge to improve the education sector ("Rural Teachers Demand Payment" 2020). Second, Dafang citizens generally have insufficient sense of the importance of education. Owing to the unaffordable tuition fees of higher education, many children were

[2] Five Measures: Including boosting the economy to provide more job opportunities, relocating poor people from inhospitable areas, compensating for economic losses associated with reducing ecological damage, improving education in impoverished areas, and providing subsistence allowances for those unable to shake off poverty through their own efforts alone.

reluctant to continue with their studies even if they had already been admitted to high schools. They worked in industries that required low or no educational background to subsidize their families after dropping out of schools (Sun 2022). Furthermore, a large-scale exodus of the labour force were seen in Guizhou due to the underdeveloped rural economy; parents could not stay in Dafang with their children. Statistics indicated that more than 4,900 children were left behind in Dafang county in 2015 ("Jiaoyu Bangfu" 2017). The lack of parents' accompany and care caused some children to quit school early and begin to make a living themselves.

The insufficient educational resources and parents' shortsightedness trapped the youth in a vicious circle, exacerbating the issues of intergenerational poverty in Dafang. In such challenging circumstances, Tongxin Vocational School, a pioneer among Dafang county's educational poverty alleviation projects, began its efforts to conquer poverty.

Tongxin School: Creating Opportunities of Vocational Training

As one of the targeted poverty educational alleviation programs implemented in Guizhou Province, Bijie Tongxin Agricultural and Industrial Secondary Vocational and Technical School (Tongxin School) opened in 2010. Encouraged by the Chinese Peasants' and Workers' Democratic Party (CPWDP), the vice chairman of the Heilongjiang provincial committees of the CPWDP, and the chairman of Sanctity Biological Pharmaceutical Ltd., Mr. Gao Xiang donated CNY 5 million for constructing this full-time technical school in Dafang County. The school set up eight practical majors and officially started admissions in September 2011. The flexibility of the curriculum allowed students to pursue fields of interest while fulfilling the requirement of vocational training. With the continuous assistance from Dafang county, CPWDP, enterprises, and various social institutions, students were exempt from tuition and accommodation fees.

Solutions

Tongxin School improved teaching quality by recruiting elite teachers from universities outside the province. Via an educational support scheme, the Chinese central government allocated over CNY 4.5 billion to improve the living standard and teaching environment of 1.27 million rural teachers in 2018. Moreover, recently graduated college students and outstanding retired teachers were encouraged to provide additional support to education in rural areas as volunteers (Ministry of Education 2019). To introduce new educational methodologies and improve the managerial ability of recruited teachers, the China Vocational Education Association, the

China Warmth Project Foundation, and other institutions also contributed and invited hundreds of educators to participate in relevant training (China Vocational Education Association 2022).

By reducing the financial burden of individual households, the school encouraged parents from low-income families to support their children to obatain higher education. Students could enjoy reduced tuition and accommodation fees with continuous support from the county government, CPWDP, and various enterprises. For instance, the Modern Vocational Education Fund of the China Warmth Project Foundation donated CNY 750,000 in November 2021 and helped 500 students with family difficulties to complete their studies (China Vocational Education Association 2022).

Along with its educational function, the school also collaborated with local government and enterprises to teach students practical skills and improve their employability. The tripartite cooperation between the school, government, and enterprises has enhanced local attention to education and offered students with better employment prospects. The school set up highly practical majors, such as nursing, automobile operation and maintenance, preschool education, hospitality operation and management, and computer application (Bijie Tongxin 2020). All aimed to provide better employment prospects and a decent income for its graduates. In addition, through the connection between the school and the enterprise platform, students could choose to continue their studies or to be recommended for employment according to their preference after graduation (State Council Information Office 2021). As a result, the willingness to learn was boosted, as the students knew that stable jobs and a considerable income increase would follow if they could graduate from the school.

Outcome: Achievements of Tongxin School

Tongxin School has consistently evolved and developed since its establishment 10 years ago, and it is recognized as a benchmark in the fields of poverty alleviation through education. In 2022, the school had 97 full-time teachers and more than 2,800 full-time students, who benefited from enjoying the well-equipped school facilities purchased with government fund (State Council Information Office 2021). It covers an area of 63.5 hectares comprising more than 12,000 m^2 of grassland, 9,500 m^2 sports field, and 43,857 m^2 building area (State Council Information Office 2021).

The high school enrolment rate in Guizhou Province increased from 55% in 2010 (Zhongguo Jiaoyu Zaixian 2016) to 91% in 2021 (Li and Liang 2022). As one of the first targeted poverty alleviation projects in Guizhou Province, Tongxin School has cultivated many talented students and transferred them to the workplace. The overall employment rate of vocational college graduates in Guizhou has risen from 30 to 70% in the last 10 years (Cheng 2021), guaranteeing technical and skill support to Guizhou's economic growth. During the past three years, Tongxin School nurtured 1,590 graduates and recommended them for more than 1,340 jobs of 36 institutions inside and outside Guizhou (State Council Information Office 2021).

Tongxin School was still functioning actively and making significant contributions to poverty alleviation progress in Guizhou Province as of 2022.

Sustainable Development Goals

Being a global advocate to terminate poverty through reversing the earth's environmental deterioration, and ensuring people worldwide can enjoy peace and prosperity, China has set out its plan to work on the UN Sustainable Development Goals (SDGs) 1–17. This case study mainly focuses on the goals of No poverty, Quality education, and reduce inequalities. A survey published by Berenberg indicated that Quality education is listed as the most important SDG, and the most investable one (ESG Office 2018). This finding corresponds to the significant efforts of the Chinese government in alleviating poverty through education.

The eradication of extreme poverty by the end of 2020 in China marks its completion of the first target in the UN 2030 Agenda for SDGs. It represents a significant contribution to the common cause of improving the living standard of the world's populations. To respond and confront the brand-new opportunities and challenges presented by the COVID-19 pandemic, the United Nations Sustainable Development Cooperation Framework (UNSDCF) cooperated with the Chinese government to tackle problems in three prioritized areas: people, planet, and prosperity (United Nations China 2022). Ideally, the attainment of SDGs will enable China to realize its vision of high-quality development and provide the foundation for international collaboration and assistance.

The UNSDGs addressed in this case are: No poverty; Quality education; Decent work and economic growth; Reduced inequalities; and Sustainable cities and communities.

Environmental, Social, and Governance

Environmental, social, and governance (ESG) goals provide a framework for stakeholders to determine how an organization manages the sustainability of the risks and opportunities which are created by shifts in circumstances, notably, changes in environment, social, and economic systems. The criteria established by ESG can be aligned with the No poverty SDG in devising feasible strategies to alleviate poverty (Sahota 2020). In this context, Tongxin School ensured the economic well-being of disadvantageous youth by equipping them with vocational skills. From the social perspective, it released the financial burden of the rural families by reducing children's tuition fees for higher education and increasing household incomes by providing better job opportunities. In terms of governance, the establishment of a public-financed educational institution sets the standards of a systemic vocational training program.

The pillars of social and governance factors are frequently mentioned in poverty elimination, however the environmental aspect is also needed, as the long-run completion of the mission requires the sustainability of the earth. The educational approach taken by the Guizhou provincial government deserves commendation as it teaches the villagers to avoid proposals that could lead to resource over-exploitation.

Case Analysis

The theoretical framework of the PEST analysis model (political, economic, social, and technological) is often used to analyze the impact of external environment on the competitiveness of an organization. Although this model is mainly used to develop business strategies for firms, it can also identify the risks and opportunities presented by the establishment of Tongxin School in reducing poverty in Dafang County (Six Sigma n.d.).

Political

Based on a categorization by Tanya Sammut-Bonnici, there are three main dimensions of political factors, the supernational, the national, and the subnational levels (Sammut-Bonnici and Galea 2014). Supernational organizations and communities such as the World Bank and the United Nations strive to eradicate poverty, calling for governments to address the "ethical, social, political and economic imperative of mankind" (Department of Economic and Social Affairs n.d.). The No poverty target being endorsed as the Millennium Development Goal 1 in the Millennium Summit also demonstrates the significance of poverty alleviation in terms of formulating a common mission and setting a crucial criterion for governments and policymakers.

The political factors are the most important component among the four since poverty elimination is a crucial political commitment of the ruling party and requires the will and effort of all the citizens. Without the motivation and support of the highest political authority, the financial and human resources required in the construction of the school cannot be coordinated and assigned to rural areas in such an efficient and well-organized manner. As long as the No poverty goal remains on the agenda of the international community, there will be more vocational training schools like Tongxin planned and built across the rural areas of China.

Economic

Various schools of economists have affirmed that long-run economic development cannot exist without deliberate investment in human capital (Schultz 1961). The rapidly growing and dynamic economy of China since the reform and opening-up seems a miracle to the world, yet the puzzle can be easily explained by its enormous input in the education sector. In return, the booming economy provides sufficient funds for expanding people's access of educational facilities to those suffering financially. Besides the construction of vocational training centers like Tongxin School, the Chinese government also fund-raises for the tuition waivers, financial aids, and scholarships for those in need, fulfilling its commitment of "leaving no children behind" (Liu et al. 2021).

The cultivation of young, talented students not only lifts individual households out of poverty, but also lays foundation for economic development on a national level. As illustrated in the white book released by the Chinese government, the goals of eradicating poverty and building a moderately prosperous society are inextricably linked. These two parts play a crucial role in sustaining the current uptrend of the economy. The rapidly growing economy of China was slightly interrupted by the COVID-19 pandemic in 2019. The closure of international market and supply chain disruption has no doubt been the most disruptive factor to China's economy since the 2008 economic crisis (Elms 2021). Despite the government's lockdown measures, most of the schools adopted online teaching or closed-loop management and continued to teach their students. During the shutdown periods caused by the pandemic, the transformation of working from offline to online indicated that a large, versatile, and well-educated labour force is the key to economic survival of every country.

Social

The monitoring and evaluation of social factors render a clear picture of the needs and expectation of different groups of stakeholders. An analytical approach called Poverty and Social Impact Analysis (PSIA) is widely applied to assess the distributional impacts of the amendments and reforms of policies on society, particularly on vulnerable and impoverished groups (World Bank n.d.). Even the best-planned policies have their pros and cons, which should be identified and amended before they are implemented. For example, although the exemption from tuition fees allows more low-income families to send their children to school, the financial and human resources wielded by the school system may also be limited, preventing it from further expansion to admit more students.

Poverty alleviation through education also addresses the inequality issue between urban and rural areas and helps national minorities to get involved in the social mainstream. It is common that parents in the mountain areas were unaware of the benefits of higher education. Therefore, they are indifferent and even reluctant to finance their children's schooling. The young people in rural areas are mainly deprived of the skills and knowledge required for employment compared to those raised in the cities. Thus, a self-perpetuating poverty trap forms and is continuously reinforced. The solution presented by the case study, which is to extend free public education to impoverished areas, mobilized young people from impoverished family backgrounds to pursue vocational education and possibly start their own businesses. Moreover, eradicating extreme poverty in remote regions granted the young people in these areas a better starting point which allows them to compete fairly with their urban counterparts. Tongxin School also created a platform for the widely distributed ethnic minorities to blend with the dominant Han population by interacting and communicating in both school and workplace. Their assimilation into the mainstream society reduces the social costs associated with ethnic conflicts and cultural clashes, enhancing the effectiveness of poverty alleviation policies.

Technological

Last, the recent breakthroughs in technology and its application in education sectors has proved to be beneficial and effective as the teaching process has become more engaging and convenient. As Tongxin School acquires more teaching facilities and resources, the gap between young people who live in urban and rural areas will gradually get narrowed. Education is arguably the most important propellant to technological advancement in industries. One of the most important purposes of Tongxin School is to equip youth with an entrepreneurial and innovative mindset, which enable them to become more competitive in job markets.

Best Practice Case: Poverty Alleviation and Wealth Creation Evening School empowered by TV Broadcast in Hainan

The Hainan provincial government established a task force for the Poverty Alleviation and Wealth Creation Evening School with TV broadcast (TV evening school) and the TV evening school programs have been airing since November 2016, aiming at impoverished farmers with low educational levels. Their series of television programs cover practical information such as housing, education, medical services, and micro-credit. Each episode of "Rural Classroom" invited government officials and agricultural experts to share their experiences and perspectives on productivity improvement, wealth management, and technological innovation. Villagers could also learn about the poverty alleviation policies available in their province. As of June 2020, Hainan province had over 2,700 teaching centers supported by thousands of personnel from government and industry. The weekly live programs attracted an average of about 680,000 viewers per episode.

To amplify the impact of the TV evening school, various online and offline supplementary activities were organized. Firstly, a TV evening school hotline call center was established to direct viewers' inquiries to experienced personnel in the region. They addressed the inquiries individually with specific and effective solutions within the week. Secondly, local forums at villages were initiated for impoverished households to discuss paths out of poverty, with experts providing consultation services on topics like agriculture, forestry, etc. Thirdly, quizzes on related topics and competitions with prizes were held to serve as an incentive to further raise villagers' interest in participating in the learning programs.

Encouraged by their learning, the villagers actively participated in training to enhance their practical skills, essential for helping impoverished farmers break free from their current situation. Inspired by the programs, they have developed their businesses in various forms, such as cooperatives for animal husbandry, successfully lifting themselves out of poverty.

International Comparative Studies

The international applications of poverty alleviation policies in other countries can serve as a reference in terms of their feasibility globally and inspire exchange of practical experiences.

A paper published in the *British Journal of Arts and Social Sciences* reports on the significance of education in driving economic development and thereby reducing poverty in the real-world scenario of Nigeria (Omoniyi 2013). The article states that according to estimates of the United Nations Development Project (UNDP) in 2010, around 93% of the population living in extreme poverty mainly resided in the East Asia, South Asia, and Sub-Saharan Africa. In the lack of proper shelter, nutrition, and water resources, National Bureau of Statistics (NBS) reports in 2019 highlighted that 83 million of Nigerians, or 40% of its total population, were living below the country's poverty line of 137.43 naira (USD 381.75) per person per year (World Bank 2020). The main reason to severe poverty includes both periodic and systematic dimensions. First, the roads and infrastructures in Nigeria are often eroded by seasonal rain, and the lack of access to health services attenuates the spread of endemic diseases. Second, structural poverty generally passes down from generation to generation as the parents can hardly maintain a livelihood in large families of five or six children. It thus become impossible for the children to receive higher education. The lack of fundamental education has been a root cause to the trap of endless poverty, especially in the rural areas.

Given the complexities and dynamics of Nigeria's poverty, the strategic framework set up for sustainable development centered on empowering the citizens in skill acquisition and youth empowerment. Capacity enhancement programs were conducted in various forms, including a microcredit curriculum and vocational training centers (Cross River 2019). These schemes were developed to empower the villagers, especially the youth, by enabling them to realize their visions and providing them with material safety.

Despite the recent campaigns on poverty alleviation, an assessment by the World Bank revealed that tackling poverty would remain a challenge to Nigeria as it also confronts a wide range of development challenges. The conservative prediction is that 5 million more population will be pushed into poverty due to the impact of the COVID-19 pandemic and surging inflation rate (World Bank 2022).

Comparing the measures taken by the Nigerian government and the Tongxin School may better illustrate the preconditions for alleviating poverty through education.

First, the establishment and maintenance of public educational institutions require an effective central government, and the duties of each level of executive agencies need to be clearly defined. Regarding the government's efforts to improve public education programs, the report emphasizes the coordination difficulties in effective allocation of national resources. In Nigeria, the most basic elements of education, such as setting standards, rest with the federal government, while most of the public services are implemented by the sub-national levels of authorities, in particular, the state and local governments. The decentralized social system in Nigeria appeared to be less effective than the top-down administrative style operated in China in devising and actualizing a coherent national strategy.

Before considering the reform and improvement of its educational sector, the availability of public funding to finance the projects needs to be evaluated. In this case, the relatively weak economic foundation of Nigeria should be recognized as a main reason for its inability to invest consistently in education as the COVID-19 pandemic further weakened its export industries. The enlarging disparities in infrastructure, the provision of municipal services, and income per capita between the two countries may also explain why poverty alleviation through education is more appropriate in China than Nigeria. The latter has been harder hit by the economic crisis caused by the COVID-19 pandemic due to Nigeria's reliance on oil exports. Accelerating inflation and the increased costs of consumption goods have exacerbated long-standing structural poverty. In comparison with China, the current economic underperformance makes it much more difficult for Nigeria to invest in education, the benefits of which may not be observed in short time.

Looking Forward: Creating Opportunities for International Collaboration

Investing in education undeniably has a long-lasting effect on poverty alleviation, especially intergenerational poverty. However, it demands a massive amount of financial and human resources as the starting foundation and its outcomes may take years to become evident. Concerning these characteristics, poverty alleviation through education might not be an optimal or constructive solution for developing countries which don't possess adequate educational resources while prioritizing economic growth. However, in the current world, there are numerous potential collaboration opportunities which provide developing countries with both financial and technological support. The future opportunities for international collaboration are full of possibility and a large space for development. With support from the United Nations, developed nations, and other charity organizations, sufficient resources like learning and training materials, and smart hardware, can be allocated to the countries in need.

As the world's largest developing country, China is always willing to build international friendly relationship and to collaborate with other developing countries to achieve a win–win outcome. Moreover, after years of poverty alleviation practice, China has experience and resources and has successfully eliminated extreme poverty by the end of 2020. We believe that with international cooperation and mutual understanding between China and other developing countries, more educational poverty alleviation projects can be launched and play a more important role in the common mission of poverty reduction.

References

Bijie Tongxin Nonggong Zhongdeng Zhiye Jishu Xuexiao 毕节同心农工中等职业技术学校 [Bijie Tongxin Agricultural and Industrial Secondary Vocational and Technical School]. (2020, May 19). *Xuexiao jianjie 学校简介* [Brief introduction on the school]. Retrieved October 19, 2022, from http://www.bjtxngzx.cn/article.php?aid=360

Cheng, T. (2021, November 20). *Guizhou Sheng Jiaoyuting tingzhang: Jin wu nian Guizhou zhongzhi biyesheng chuci jiuyelv chao jiushiwu 贵州省教育厅厅长:近5年贵州中职毕业生初次就业率超95%* [Chairman of Education Bureau in Guizhou Province: In the past five years, the initial employment rate of secondary vocational graduates in Guizhou has exceeded 95%]. Pengpai Xinwen. https://www.thepaper.cn/newsDetail_forward_15478049

China Vocational Education Association. (2022, January 18). *Qingqing zhijiao gongyi shiye zhutui Bijie shiyanqu fazhan 情倾职教公益事业 助推毕节试验区发展* [Sincere vocational education public welfare to boost the development of Bijie pilot zone]. http://zhzjs.org.cn/wngc/94009.jhtml

Cross River State Ministry of Finance. (2019). *Rural poverty reduction and sustainable development in Nigeria.*

Department of Economic and Social Affairs. (n.d.). *Poverty eradication*. United Nations. Retrieved October 31, 2022, from https://apastyle.apa.org/style-grammar-guidelines/references/examples/webpage-website-references#3

Elms, D. (2021). Trade disrupted: Global tensions, US-China trade war and COVID-19 impact. In Singh, D. & Cook, M. (Eds.), *Southeast Asian Affairs 2021* (pp. 39–52). ISEAS Publishing. https://doi.org/10.1355/9789814951753

ESG Office. (2018, December). *Understanding the SDGs in sustainable investing*. Berenberg Bank. https://www.berenberg.de/files/ESG%20News/SDG_understanding_SDGs_in_sustainable_investing.pdf

Guiyang Poverty Alleviation Office (2021). *China's solution for precise poverty alleviation: The case of Guizhou* (1st ed.). People's Publishing House.

Jiaoyu bangfu zoujin Dafang 教育帮扶走进大方 [Poverty alleviation through education in Dafang]. (2017, March 7). *Jinri Zhongguo* [China Today]. http://www.chinatoday.com.cn/spc/2017-03/07/content_737188.htm

Li, L. & Yang, J. (2020, September 8). Guizhou's efforts cut school dropout rate. *China Daily*. https://www.chinadailyhk.com/hk/article/142528#Guizhou's-efforts-cut-school-dropout-rate

Li, Z., & Liang, Z. (2022, October 10). "Lianglv" shou chao quanguo, Guizhou jiaoyu shiye anxia "kuaijin jian" "两率"首超全国 贵州教育事业按下"快进键" ["Two rates" surpassed the whole country for the first time, and Guizhou's education industry pressed the "fast forward button"]. *Guizhou Ribao* [Guizhou Daily]. https://new.qq.com/rain/a/20221010A03ISK00

Liangmian yibu 两免一补 [Two exemptions and one subsidy plan]. (2022, November 7). In *Wikipedia*. https://zh.wikipedia.org/w/index.php?title=%E4%B8%A4%E5%85%8D%E4%B8%80%E8%A1%A5&oldid=63176478

Liu, C., Xu, K., & Liu, X. (2021, November 1). China's heavy investment in education lays foundation for national development. *Global Times*. https://www.globaltimes.cn/page/202111/1237852.shtml

Mandela, Nelson (1990, June 23) *Speech at Madison Park High School, Boston*; reported in various forms

Ministry of Education, China. (2019, February 16). *China makes efforts to nurture teaching staff in rural areas*. http://en.moe.gov.cn/news/media_highlights/201902/t20190219_370143.html#:~:text=In%202018%2C%20China%20recruited%20over%2085%2C000%20college%20graduates,teach%20in%20rural%20areas%20by%20providing%20government-financed%20education

Omoniyi, M. B. I. (2013). The role of education in poverty alleviation and economic development: A theoretical perspective and counselling implications. *British Journal of Arts and Social Sciences, 15*(2), 176–185.

Rural teachers demand payment of millions of yuan in wage arrears. (2020, October 5). *China Labour Bulletin*. https://clb.org.hk/en/content/rural-teachers-demand-payment-millions-yuan-wage-arrears

Sahota, P. (2020, June 29). The 'no poverty' goal & ESG. *Equilibrium ProRisk*. https://equilibriumprorisk.org/2020/06/29/the-no-poverty-goal-esg/

Sammut-Bonnici, T., & Galea, D. (2014). Pest Analysis. In Cooper, C. L. (Ed.). *Wiley Encyclopedia of Management*. Wiley.

Schultz, T. W. (1961). Investment in Human Capital. *The American Economic Review, 51*(1), 1–17. http://www.jstor.org/stable/1818907

Shi'er nian yiwu jiaoyu 十二年义务教育 [12-year compulsory education]. (2022, November 7). In *Baidu Encyclopedia*. https://baike.baidu.com/item/%E5%8D%81%E4%BA%8C%E5%B9%B4%E4%B9%89%E5%8A%A1%E6%95%99%E8%82%B2/6973443

Six Sigma Training Free Site. (n.d.). *Pest Analysis*. Retrieved October 31, 2022, from https://www.sixsigmatrainingfree.com/pest-analysis.html

State Council Information Office of the People's Republic of China (2021). *Poverty alleviation: China's experience and contribution* (1st ed.). Foreign Language Press. Retrieved October 19, 2022, from http://www.xinhuanet.com/english/download/2021-4-6/FullText.pdf

Sun, Y. (2022). *Investigating on targeted poverty alleviation campaign in China: Case study of Guizhou Province* [Master's thesis, Lund University]. Lund University Publications Student Papers. http://lup.lub.lu.se/student-papers/record/9092416

The Viewport of Dafang in Guizhou, China. (2022). *People's Daily*.

United Nations Association of Australia. (2017, June 28). *UNESCO study reveals correlation between poverty and education*. https://www.unaa.org.au/2017/06/28/unesco-study-reveals-correlation-between-poverty-and-education/

United Nations China. (n.d.). *The sustainable development goals in China*. Retrieved October 19, 2022, from https://china.un.org/en/sdgs

World Bank. (2020, May 28). *Nigeria releases new report on poverty and inequality in country*. https://www.worldbank.org/en/programs/lsms/brief/nigeria-releases-new-report-on-poverty-and-inequality-in-country

World Bank. (2022, March 22). *Nigeria poverty assessment 2022: A better future for all Nigerians*. World Bank. https://www.worldbank.org/en/news/infographic/2022/03/21/afw-nigeria-poverty-assessment-2022-a-better-future-for-all-nigerians

World Bank. (n.d.). *Poverty and social impact analysis (PISA)*.

Zhongguo Jiaoyu Zaixian. (2016, November 10). *Zhongguo Jiaoyu Zaixian zhuanfang Guizhou Jiaoyuting tingzhang Wang Fengyou: "Xiangzhen shang zuihao de jianzhu yiding shi xuexiao" 中国教育在线专访贵州教育厅厅长王凤友:"乡镇上最好的建筑一定是学校"* [Interview with Wang Fengyou, director of Guizhou Education Department: "The best building in a town must be a school"]. https://guizhou.eol.cn/guizhounews/201611/t20161110_1466560.shtml

Cultural and Tourism Development at Menggen Village

In Targeted Poverty Alleviation (TPA, 精准扶贫), one of the strategies was cultural poverty alleviation. In March 2014, the Ministry of Culture and the Ministry of Finance jointly issued the Master Plan for the development of the Tibetan–Qiang–Yi Cultural Industry Corridor (藏羌彝文化走廊), which includes seven provinces and autonomous regions: Sichuan, Guizhou, Yunnan, Tibet, Shaanxi, Jiangxi, and Qinghai. They are the core areas of China's poverty alleviation. This showed the government's intention to alleviate cultural poverty. In addition to traditional cultural factors, such as folk songs and dances, intangible cultural heritage is gradually being taken into account in poverty alleviation policies. In 2018, after its establishment, the Ministry of Culture and Tourism issued a notice on the vigorous revitalization of traditional crafts in poor areas to help alleviate poverty. In recent years, many places have been exploring and practicing "intangible heritages + poverty alleviation" to help alleviate poverty, and this have achieved remarkable results.

After the success of the 13th Five-Year Plan, the communiqué of the Fifth Central Committee of CPC stated: "Cultural self-confidence will be gradually established by the vast number of poor areas and the poor people. And the cultural self-confidence of poor people will make China's cultural self-confidence more complete." Menggen village (勐根村) is one of the best examples of building cultural self-confidence in poor areas. Menggen village, which is in Jiujing Hani Ethnic Township, Yucang Lahu Autonomous County, Pu'er City, Yunnan Province, has a population of 481 people and 116 households. The villagers relied mainly on watermelon and tea for income. However, with the rapid development of science and technology, Menggen village gradually fell behind. For example, transportation and other infrastructure in the village were seriously outdated, the farmers' income structure was too simple, and they lacked scientific and technological awareness. Instead, they had been using traditional agriculture which relies on nature, instead of modern technology. Facing these challenges, in 2013 the village committee had to consider how to leverage

International Poverty Reduction Center In China, *Poverty Alleviation Case Analysis In China*, SpringerBriefs on Case Studies of Sustainable Development,
https://doi.org/10.1007/978-981-97-4537-1_5

the folk culture to help the villages generate more income. The village management decided to focus on developing the *Laodabao* (老达保) culture of Menggen village to attract tourists. At the same time, in order to establish a relatively complete cultural industry chain to attract tourists, they developed primary and secondary industries as well.

Focal Issue

Cultural Poverty Alleviation

In addition to the traditional methods of poverty alleviation, such as improving productivity, the Chinese government also carried out a poverty alleviation program which focused on the culture in the Menggen village, where the villagers largely belong to the *Lahu* (拉祜) minority group. There are many definitions of cultural poverty alleviation, and the concept adopted in Menggen Village means recognizing and effectively utilizing the cultural resources in poor areas. This includes both importing and exporting. Importing is the construction of education and public facilities in poor areas with the help of other institutes, while exporting is the use of the poor areas' cultural resources to develop them into a form which can help improve the village's condition in the long term. Meanwhile, Guizhou embroidery and other handicraft have also significantly contributed to lifting local people out of poverty.

A few parties need to be introduced before analyzing the case. First are the institutions which played a role. Also, as this case is about cultural poverty alleviation, it is essential to learn about the *Lahu* minority and their *Laodabao* culture.

The Institutions

Different institutions in China helped to alleviate poverty. According to the "Outline for Poverty Alleviation and Development in Rural China (2011–2020)" issued by the Central Committee of the CPC and the State Council (2011), poverty alleviation in each region is led by the central government, while governments at all levels take overall responsibility in this issue and integrate it into their economic and social development strategies and overall planning. The local governments can cooperate with different departments. For example, the Ministry of Culture and Tourism works with the Lancang county government or the secretary of the *Laodabao* Village to plan the entire cultural poverty alleviation project. The development plan also encourages the involvement of enterprises and the community in poverty alleviation, in addition to the various government departments. For instance, in Menggen village, in addition to government officials, in 2013 the secretary of the Chinese Academy of Sciences came to the village to work with the local government authorities in 2013. It is made by applying scientific and technological knowledge to the fields. They were able to promote the development of local primary and secondary industries, which solved the problem of poverty in the village from a different perspective (Wen et al. 2020).

The Lahu People

To understand the cultural poverty alleviation in Menggen Village, it is necessary to learn about the local culture. The culture of the ethnic minorities in Menggen Village comes from the Lahu minority, one of the 55 ethnic minorities in China. The Lahu minority, which originated from the ancient Qiang people (羌族) around Gansu and Qinghai Provinces, used to live nomadic lives. Later they moved southwards with the Qiang people. Some travelled across the border to reach the mountainous regions of Burma, Vietnam, Laos, and Thailand in the central and southern Asia peninsula. At present, the total population of the Lahu minority is 485,966 (2010), 447,600 of which are in Yunnan Province. The Lahu minority in Yunnan mainly live at the western bank of the *Lancang* River (澜沧江). Lancang is the only Lahu autonomous county in China, with nearly 50% of the total Lahu population (National Ethnic Affairs Commission n.d.).

In the language of these people, "la" means tiger and "hu" means roasting meat. Thus, historically, the Lahu minority were known as the "tiger-hunting people." They live in mountainous areas and call themselves "mountain people". Thus, their villages are usually built on the tops of hills and halfway up the mountains. The Lahu people are good at singing and dancing, especially during festivals, when they sing and dance to celebrate. The dances range from those which reflect production and life to those that simulate animal movements, and many which reflect rituals, such as the Prayer Dance and the New Year Worship. These talents in arts have provided the basis for the subsequent path of cultural poverty alleviation (National Ethnic Affairs Commission n.d.).

Laodabao

Dabao was the name of a Lahu tribal leader. This tough chief led his people across the mountains and into the primeval forest in the middle reaches of the Lancang River, where he gradually built the village. This stockade village, in Menggen, was officially named *Laodabao* in honor of his contribution.

However, the development of the village lagged behind other places of Lancang county. The village is in the southeast of Lancang County, with a distance of 42 km from the county center. It is one of the bases for the protection and transmission of the national intangible cultural heritage "*Mupamipa*" (牡帕密帕), the Lahu epic of creation, and is where the Lahu folk song "Happy Lahu" is sung. The 402 people who lived in the village had a poverty rate of 79%. Laodabao had poor land, weak industrial base, and seriously lagging infrastructures such as transportation and water conservancy. People still made a living by praying for good weather and without any help from modern technology. Therefore, it was hard for the local farmers to increase their income (International Poverty Reduction Centre in China [IPRCC] 2021). Many villagers had never gone out of the mountains in their lifetime. Someone described the situation in the village as "the dust flew on sunny days, the roads were slippery on rainy days, and it is inaccessible by any means of transportations" (Yang 2020).

There is much potential for development in Laodabao village. Taking the local culture as an example, all of the over 100 families in Laodabo village are Lahu people, and all have retained their distinctive Lahu skills. The villagers, from the elderly to the children, are all excellent singers and dancers, specializing in dances of their culture and singing a cappella. Moreover, 80% of the villagers can play guitar, and more than 70% know the traditional skills of the Lahu minority. In addition, traditional Lahu spinning and weaving have been preserved and perpetuated, which can be traced back more than 600 years. With these treasures inherited from their ancestors, the villagers of Laodabao were able to lift themselves out of poverty and onto the road to prosperity (Li 2022a, b).

Challenges

Overview

There were three main challenges facing the poverty alleviation project in Laodabao village: first, the industrial structure was simple and relied excessively on unstable and low-yielding agriculture. Second, the infrastructure in the village was quite poor. Third were the ideological and cultural factors.

Simple Industrial Structure

Farming was the main industry of Laodabao village. The village consisted of 114 households and 291 laborers, 246 of whom were engaged in the primary industry. However, the plantation industry is characterized by heavy dependence on the weather and extensive planting with thin harvest. The primary sector is vulnerable to natural disasters, market conditions, and epidemics, when happened, it could take a long time for the sector to recover. These have made their income highly unstable. In addition, Laodabao village's agricultural products were homogeneous and low yielding, as reported by Peng Na'er, secretary of the Laodabao Party branch, "at that time, we grew tea, sugar cane and corn, which are not profitable." Therefore, the traditional source of income hindered the villagers in escaping poverty.

Backward Infrastructure

Second, the undeveloped infrastructure of transportation and water conservancy posed serious obstacle for Laodabao. In the past, this village was a place where, traveling mainly on foot, people fetched water from rivers. By the end of 2010, the village road was still dirt, and the main road, which was unhardened, was 3 km from the nearest bus station and 3 km to the nearest market. As Laodabao's agricultural products needed to be sold to the county, its poor transportation facilities greatly affected local trade. In addition, its water facilities were relatively poor, limiting local agricultural development. Thus, poor infrastructure was a major challenge for Laodabao Village in escaping poverty.

Traditional Ideology and Culture

Third, ideology and culture were also essential. On the one hand, farmers' low awareness of science and technology led to a low level of agricultural technology input, which had affected agricultural development. On the other hand, villagers were bound by the traditional ideology of living off the land and had a serious mind-set of retaining the status quo. As Hu Hong, the first secretary of the Kunming Branch of the Chinese Academy of Sciences in Menggen village, said, "In the past, Laodabao was a typical poor village in the mountainous areas of ethnic minorities, with a serious lag in transportation, water conservancy, and other infrastructure facilities. Local people were bound by traditional ideology of living off the land and planting a wide range of crops, which make it difficult for people to increase their income." Thus, the industrial structure which relies solely on agriculture, backward infrastructure, and the traditional ideology and culture were the challenges encountered by the local community in fighting poverty.

Solutions

To address these challenges, different departments tried to solve the dilemma that Menggen Village, which includes Laodabo in its region, is facing. To improve the villagers' industrial structure, the poverty alleviation department is working on two aspects: using science and technology to change the local farmers' cultivation and using the traditional culture of Laodabo to develop tourism. Both aspects require educating local people to alter their outdated mindset in farming and their culture.

Changing People's Minds About Agriculture

The first step of changing the industrial structure is to change the mindset of the villagers. Comrade Hu Hong, a poverty alleviation expert who was sent by the Kunming Branch of the Chinese Academy of Sciences and the first secretary of Menggen village, has applied the technology of the Chinese Academy of Sciences to the cultivation of Menggen village. Hu Hong and the village cadres mobilized the villagers and helped to solve the problem from each step in planting, picking, selling, and dividing watermelons. When these actions bring benefits, the villagers can also be inspired, and more people are willing to participate in technical reforms in agriculture.

In addition to watermelon cultivation, Hu Hong tried to foster villagers' enthusiasm for other aspects of production. From the year 2015 to 2020, with the support of the Chinese Academy of Sciences, Hu Hong took village cadres and villagers out of Menggen village to "learn from the experience" and introduce new planting products and production techniques. By observing business timing, the party members took the lead in sowing crops which were in high demand outside Menggen village. This motivated everyone to participate through real returns. As for technology, in 2017, Hu Hong learned about organizational operations while encouraging folks to start a cooperative. He also invited experts to the village to conduct several practical technical trainings around local development needs. In addition, through the resources of the Chinese Academy of Sciences, Hu Hong led the villagers to apply the fertilizer efficiency technology of Zhong Naiqin, a researcher at the Institute of Microbiology of the Chinese Academy of Sciences in Beijing, to sugarcane cultivation, and to extend the 20-hectare experimental field of sugarcane to 749 hectares (Wen et al. 2020).

In addition to agriculture, the poverty alleviation department also strengthened local tourism. To develop tourism, transportation facilities are essential. Fortunately, the China–Laos Railway (also known as Boten–Vientiane Railway) was put into use on 3 December 2021, so travellers from all over the country can easily travel to Yunnan by railway. To develop tourism in Menggen village, various departments helped the poor in the following ways (IPRCC 2021).

Combination of Ethnic Characteristic Villages and Poverty Alleviation and Development

With its own advantages of ethnic cultural resources, Menggen village has mobilized more than CNY 32.5 million of funds for projects such as thatched-roof house renovation, characteristic villages, new ecological song and dance performance square, improved village tour roads, tourist toilets, electricity, drainage, and other infrastructure. The fund was also used to implement "cultural farms" which include viewing pavilions, experience houses, and handmade grill houses. Further, a Lahu cultural heritage museum and display areas for Lahu ethnic folklore and a farming culture such as the Lusheng workshop and the gyro workshop were also built.

Integration of Heritage and Development

Laodabao village promotes the transformation of ethnic cultural resources into the advantages of poverty alleviation through tourism. The party branch of Laodabo has established a system of party members contacting households and formed 11 "party members of the cultural team + the public" pairs with masters leading their apprentices and elders leading their juniors to improve the skills of the public in cultural performance and etiquette. The group has mastered more than 70% of traditional Lahu skills and more than 80% of vocational skills. In 2013, Laodabao established a cultural and performing company, Lancang Laodabao Happy Lahu Performing Arts Co. The company has created a live-action drama, and the income from the performance has become one of the most important channels to increase the income of the 90 households and 398 poor families in the group.

Education and Learning as Well as Skills Enhancement

Relying on the intellectual advantages of the Kunming Branch of the Chinese Academy of Sciences, the party members continued to strengthen support for poverty alleviation industries. This was achieved through various initiatives, including lecture on the battle against poverty (脱贫攻坚决战冲刺大讲堂), firepit night school (火塘夜校), and skills training (技能培训). These educational platforms were combined with practical technical training in areas such as tea garden transformation, planting, and breeding. The aim was to improve the quality and efficiency of traditional industries such as tea and animal husbandry. Additionally, efforts were made to actively develop emerging industries like handicraft production, ethnic catering, and bed and breakfast inns. This comprehensive approach aimed to uplift impoverished communities and drive sustainable economic growth. At the same time, with the support of the Chinese Academy of Sciences, Hu Hong actively promoted the construction of an elementary school science education demonstration base, the Menggen Village Elementary School Library, the "Jiujing Township High School Science and Technology Museum" for education, learning and the skills enhancement.

Case Analysis

Overview

First, to ensure the sustainability of income from the tertiary sector, the tourist industry based on local culture, simultaneous development of all the three sectors is essential. Also, in addition to the economic aspect of poverty alleviation, the psychological aspect of cultural identity is important, and the cultural approach to poverty alleviation in Menggen village has helped villagers to build their self-confidence in the local culture and thus improve self-recognition.

Important Concepts

In the development of the primary, secondary, and tertiary industries, the primary sector is agriculture, forestry, animal husbandry, and fishery. The secondary sector is mining, manufacturing, electricity, gas and water production and supply, and construction. The tertiary sector is the industries other than the primary and secondary sectors, which is mainly the service industry (National Bureau of Statistics of China 2022).

The second important concept is cultural identity, the consensus and recognition of people's inclination toward culture, which has a great effect on individuals, society, nations, and countries. It is the source of an individual's sense of belonging and an important reason for the formation of a social group (Zuo and Wen 2017).

Economic Development by Sectors

Most countries have achieved economic prosperity by developing the primary sector, followed by the secondary, and finally the tertiary. But the current situation is that even developed countries, whose economies largely relying on tertiary industries, have not completely abandoned the secondary sector. This is because the primary and secondary sectors serve as the cornerstone for the development of the tertiary sector. In the case of the village of Menggen, its path of poverty alleviation demonstrates the simultaneous development of all three industries. While the Laodabo culture contributes to the development of tourism, i.e. tertiary sector, the government also focuses on other sectors at the same time. For instance, a significant portion of funds is allocated to infrastructure construction, including the construction of toilets, electricity and drainage systems, and the housing projects.

At the same time, the Chinese railway authorities have been working to make trains available in these areas, resulting in the completion of the Lao–China Railway in 2021. As a result, tourists can easily access Menggen village and enjoy a comfortable journey. In the long run, the tourism industry in Laodabao is expected to attract more visitors in the long run. Additionally, experts from the Chinese Academy of Sciences have assisted with crops cultivation in Menggen Village to ensure the viability of the village's crops. Therefore, it can be observed that overcoming poverty relies on the substantial income generated by the tertiary sector, which is only possible with the foundation of the primary and secondary industries (Zhang 2021).

Cultural Identity

Menggen is a village where poverty has been overcome by the culture of local community. During the alleviation process, the villagers had to learn the traditional skills. As mentioned, more than 70% of the villagers in the group had mastered traditional Lahu skills by the time the project was implemented, and this learning process helped the villagers to identify their own culture.

In addition, the performance of these skills helped lift the villagers out of poverty. For example, the local company's live theatre has received more than 120,000 visitors, with revenues of CNY 4.07 million and a dividend of CNY 3.25 million, which is an important source of income for the villagers. This income would help them to improve the sense of their own culture. At the same time, some studies have shown that factors such as the evaluation of minority groups and the relationship between minority groups and other social groups can affect self-esteem and therefore their identity status (IPRCC 2021). Therefore, after the performance, the visitors' praise for their culture improves the local population's self-esteem. Both the economic development and the psychological factor helped to achieve the cultural confidence mentioned in the 13th Five Year Plan, as well as alleviation from poverty overall.

Connection to SDG/ECG

The cultural poverty alleviation project in Menggen village also meets several SDG goals. Menggen village meets several of the UN's 17 SDG goals: 1. No poverty; 5. Gender equality; 8. Decent work and economic growth; 9. Industry, innovation, and infrastructure; and 10. Reduced inequalities.

SDG1: No Poverty

Laodabao has been successfully lifted out of poverty through the implementation of the cultural poverty eradication policy. In 2018, Laodabao was selected for the UN's "China Poverty Alleviation Achievement Exhibition." By 2019, the village's total rural economic income reached CNY 5.4 million, with a per capita disposable income of CNY 11,240. This resulted in 398 individuals from 90 households being lifted out of poverty. By 2021, Laodabao's total rural economic income had reached CNY 10.678 million, with a per capita disposable income of CNY 14,595, marking an impressive "one-step leap of a thousand years," i.e., 8.5 times higher than 2016 (CNY 1,715) This signifies the successful eradication of poverty in Laodabao.

SDG5: Gender Equality

Many women were involved in the cultural poverty eradication project in Laodabo village, leading to their escape from poverty. One local woman, Li Na-xs, seized the opportunity and became the vice president of the local Laodabao Happy Lahu Performing Arts Company, which contributed to poverty eradication for the local villagers. Furthermore, the company's hostess, Li Yulan, obtained an annual income of over CNY 20,000 with the support of the company, lifting her family out of poverty. Li Xiuzhen, the director of the local women's group, obtaining an annual income of CNY 40,000 through the project, successfully overcame poverty. These examples demonstrate that the cultural poverty alleviation project in Laodabao not only provided opportunities for local women to escape poverty, but also ensure their active involvement in all projects, promoting gender equality (SDG5).

SDG8: Decent Work and Economic Growth

In this poverty alleviation project, Laodabao Village made use of its ethnic culture to develop cultural tourism, which subsequently supported the agricultural development. This strategy has created suitable job opportunities and fostered economic growth to the area. The "company + farmer" model was utilized to establish income growth while also ensuring that farming work was not affected. This model ensures a stable source of income for the local community. Local resident Zhang Zaxi shared, "I work in the vegetable garden, where I can work from home and learn valuable skills in my own field. My monthly income has increased by CNY 3,000, and I have a brighter future ahead." Through this model, local tourism has generated a combined income exceeding CNY 11 million, with the public achieving over CNY 4 million in dividends and bringing in over CNY 1 million for the local accommodation industry. Thus, the poverty alleviation project in Laodabao Village aligns with the characteristics of SDG8.

SDG9: Industry, Innovation, and Infrastructure

In 2022, under the leadership of the party branch of Laodabao Village, the local enterprise adopted the development model of "branch + company + base + farmers" to establish the Laodabao vegetable garden. Collaborating with a team of professors from Yunnan Agricultural University, they transformed idle winter fields into a scientific and technological demonstration garden, establishing "land transfer + base labor + quality improvement + industrial prosperity." This endeavor brought scientific and technological innovation and transformation to the local farmland. In addition, the local enterprise also spearheaded the construction of the Ethnic Culture Heritage Hall, the villagers' group activity room, the village stage, the performance pavilion, and eight ethnic product display areas showcasing the traditional characteristics of the Lahu ethnic group. The village has been transformed into a place of ethnic culture, leisure, and agricultural tourism. With the support of the poverty alleviation project, numerous infrastructure and tourism facilities were established in the village. Therefore, the practices in Laodabao Village met the goals of SDG9.

SDG10: Reduced Inequalities

The local party branch is committed to considering the well-being of the entire village, ensuring inclusivity for all residents. In this project, the Lancang Laodabao Happy Lahu Performing Arts Company Limited was established in 2013. It led 200 residents to become shareholders. The company distributed 95% of its income as dividends to the villagers, fostering a community characterized by joint hearts and minds According to statistics, in recent years, the local people has received CNY 4 million in dividends, and the annual per capita dividend of the performers was CNY 19,793. The local community has jointly participated in the poverty alleviation project and enjoyed economic rewards, contributing to common prosperity and reducing inequality, thereby achieving the goals of SDG10.

Best Practice Case Reference: Qufu, Shandong Province—Poverty Reduction Through Culture Development

Qufu (曲阜) is the hometown of Confucius, the birthplace of Confucian culture, and had a rural population of 252,000, with 6,673 poor households, including 13,747 people, in 2013. At that time, Qufu was facing a critical period of targeted poverty alleviation, with several problems that needed to be addressed. In terms of ideological awareness, some people had a significant sense of dependency, waiting for others to take action. In terms of conceptual change, some people lack the initiative to escape poverty themselves. In terms of family traditions, some poor people lacked the filial family tradition of respecting and loving the elderly and the honest family tradition of keeping one's word. At the same time, there were numerous harmful and traditional practices in the village which were obstacles to poverty alleviation and need to be corrected.

In response, the secretary of the Qufu Municipal Committee decided, after conducting research, to explore the contemporary value of traditional culture. The goal was to utilize the excellent local culture to educate and guide the masses, particularly those living in poverty. In practice, Qufu City has innovated and implemented the concept of "cultivating virtue, stimulating the will, and relieving hardship," (State 2020) which allowed traditional culture as a tool to help alleviate poverty.

First, building a platform was deemed an important foundational task. Relying on the 470 New Age Civilisation Practice Stations, Qufu City actively set up "one classroom and one stage"—a Confucian school in each village and a Confucian village stage. The school promotes the CPC's policies, core socialist values, and positive aspects of traditional culture through a variety of activities. At the same time, the school also organized rolling lectures and provided training in wealth-creation skills. From 2018 to 2020, the Confucius schools conducted over 1,300 lectures, which benefited more than 30,000 poor people. Furthermore, the stage hosted more than 2,600 performances. Zhou Changjian, who used to be poor, was unable to work due to a herniated disc, and his partner was in poor health as well and on medication. His two children needed money for the university, and the family mainly relied on the government's low-income guarantee to meet their basic needs. Zhou had a lot of experience in cattle raising. However, due to the worry of risks and a lack of capital, his cattle farming business never developed. Inspired by the lectures, he started to actively look for ways to get out of poverty. He used a CNY 50,000 loan to start a cattle-raising business, which brought an income of CNY 36,000 a year. Finally, he became a well-known local cattle professional. Zhou realized that happiness must be created with one's own efforts.

However, as local people's education level is low, Qufu City adopted a preaching model called "what to say, who to say, and how to say." This approach involved menu-based lecture content, a comprehensive lecture team, and the engaging lecture format. For instance, in 2018, during the performance "Complimenting our Gongjia Village" at the Confucius Academy, local poor people at Qufu City were aspired to achieve poverty alleviation. Qufu City also focused on the creation of an atmosphere of love, sincerity, filial piety, and benevolence in a courteous moral city. For example, the program of the civilized village and town promoted relieving the poor household's economic burden on "red and white affairs (红白事)," i.e., weddings and funerals, establishing women's volunteer service teams to promote healthy and hygienic habits, and recognizing exemplary individuals to stimulate confidence and determination among the masses to get out of poverty. Initiatives such as "good daughter-in-law" and "good mother-in-law," prosperous households, and civilized model households in Nishan Town's Shengyuan Village fostered an environment of upward mobility. These civilization creation and evaluation activities promoted the civilization of the village and town, so that the cultural concept of harmony and mutual help among neighbors is deeply ingrained in people's hearts.

Finally, Qufu City has a culture of filial piety and builds "one home, one canteen" to address the issue of stable poverty alleviation for the poor elderly. The "one home" aspect involves establishing village mutual aid nursing homes, following the "village mutual aid + home care" poverty alleviation model. As part of this effort, 68 village-level mutual aid nursing homes have been constructed, providing mutual care for 300 poor elderly individuals who are away from their homes but not away from their villages.

The "one canteen" aspect is the establishment of "happy canteens," guided by the principles of "government guidance, village management, and voluntary non-profit participation by villagers." These canteens serve as places where elderly individuals living in poverty can have meals and engage in social activities. It provides an avenue for communication and contribute to improving the well-being of those elderly. Additionally, Qufu City has also implemented programs such as "Quack and Talk" and "Public Opinion 5" to strengthen the effectiveness of poverty alleviation efforts. These programs aim to listen to the voices of the people, attend to their needs in terms of production and daily life, and provide assistance in times of difficulty.

In summary, Qufu City is determined to forge ahead, work hard, and remain committed to the aspirations of General Secretary Xi Jinping. They strive to fulfil the original intention and mission of building a well-off society.

International Comparative Cases

We can find many examples of cultural poverty alleviation in many other parts of the world, in addition to the Menggen village of China. For example, in the rural village of Kilimanjaro in Tanzania, tourism was developed through culture to increase the income of the local population (Anderson 2015). The situation in Kilimanjaro is very similar to that of Menggan, where farmers depended on the cultivation of agricultural products, a large part of which were seasonal crops. With the introduction of tourism related to traditional culture, the local population has not only gained a stable income, but also accessed to education and better health facilities. However, in this case, many of the villagers in Kilimanjaro had a negative attitude toward tourism development and many had very limited professional skills relating to their culture. The benefits of cultural poverty alleviation were not fully realized. We need to be aware of these areas when again implementing cultural poverty alleviation.

Another similar example comes from the Buganda region of Uganda (Ahebwa et al. 2016). This case shows how tourism based on traditional culture can improve the income of the local population by creating jobs, and also help to preserve cultural heritage sites and thus achieve sustainable development. The Buganda region in this example faced similar problems as Menggen village: How to increase the number of local visitors through tourism promotion and how to involve the local population more actively in the overall planning of the tourism project. It would be worth studying how the people in Buganda solved these issues.

Looking Forward

More Important Roles in Cultural Poverty Alleviation

Cultural poverty alleviation projects, such as the one in Laodabao, are set to play an increasingly crucial role in poverty alleviation in China. Many impoverished areas have successfully implemented cultural poverty alleviation initiatives, yielding positive outcomes. Cultural poverty alleviation not only ensures that farmers can continue their agricultural activities but also enables local residents to engage in tertiary industries such as cultural tourism, cultural services, folk craft processing, and folklore performances. This improves the local industrial structure, increases income levels, and even provides employment opportunities for disadvantaged groups, such as left-behind women. Consequently, it further promotes gender equality and achieves the goal of "enriching both pockets and heads (既要"富口袋"，也要"富脑袋")," i.e., enabling individuals to earn a good income while gaining valuable knowledge simultaneously.

Apart from Laodabao Village, Guizhou Province has driven over CNY 6 billion in industrial output and generated more than a million jobs through its non-heritage handicraft industry. Similar successful examples can be found in Nanxun and Dongxiang, located in Gansu Province. The cultural approach to poverty alleviation has proven effective in many poverty-stricken areas across China. This provides valuable insights for poverty alleviation strategies in various regions and leads to the utilization of traditional culture in more places. Nevertheless, many areas of China with cultural resources have yet to tap into their full potential. According to the survey conducted by the Jinxiu project, a collaboration between the 21st Century Business Herald (21世纪经济报道), Bohai Bank (渤海银行), and Fangtang Think Tank (方塘智库), many poor counties in several regions of China still possess untapped cultural resources which have not been effectively utilized.

Official Promotion of Cultural Poverty Alleviation

The Chinese government is increasingly emphasizing the role of culture in poverty alleviation and will encourage more such projects to adopt approaches similar to that of Laodabao Village. So far, under the leadership of the State Council's Poverty Alleviation Office and the Ministry of Culture and Tourism and the China Federation of Literary and Art Circles, culture has been integrated into poverty alleviation projects in many places of China.

By 2018, the State Council's Poverty Alleviation Office and the Ministry of Culture and Tourism jointly issued the "Notice on Supporting the Establishment of Employment Workshops for Poverty Alleviation" through Non-Foreign Heritage. This notice was to officially promote "employment workshops for poverty alleviation through intangible cultural heritage," and to encourage traditional crafts and establish many workshops with an obvious poverty-alleviation effect. In the same year, "the Notice on Vigorously Revitalising Traditional Crafts in Poverty-stricken Areas to Assist Precise Poverty Alleviation" was issued, and it also emphasized to encourage poor areas to use intangible cultural heritage to alleviate poverty and increase the revitalization of traditional culture in poor areas.

Industry-Driven Cultural Poverty Alleviation in the Future

In the future, cultural poverty alleviation will rely on industries to achieve its objectives. Previous successful cases of cultural poverty alleviation, such as Laodabao village, have demonstrated the effectiveness of local industries, such as the song and dance industry and tourism industry, in driving cultural heritage and generating income for the local community. To further this approach, 34 key cultural enterprises have been provided with support in advance in impoverished areas of Ningxia autonomous region, while 25 key projects in the cultural industry have received similar backing. Efforts have also been made to encourage the incorporation of cultural heritage, such as Hui medicine, with market development potential into tourist attractions and enterprises.

Industries play a crucial role in elevating the social status of traditional craftspeople, and with the support of cultural industries, the status and income of cultural practitioners can be enhanced. This, in turn, will inspire more individuals to engage and truly promote cultural poverty eradication in the region. Additionally, in the future, cultural poverty eradication can leverage the unique characteristics of impoverished regions to create local brands within the cultural industry. For instance, Laodabao has successfully established "Happy Lahu". By following similar approaches, future cultural poverty eradication can develop relevant industries and brands to promote local economic development and cultural heritage.

References

Ahebwa, W. M., Aporu, J. P., & Nyakaana, J. B. (2016). Bridging community livelihoods and cultural conservation through tourism: Case study of Kabaka heritage trail in Uganda. *Tourism and Hospitality Research, 16*(2), 103–115. https://doi.org/10.1177/146735841558965

Anderson, W. (2015). Cultural tourism and poverty alleviation in rural Kilimanjaro, Tanzania. *Journal of Tourism and Cultural Change, 13*(3), 208–224. https://doi.org/10.1080/14766825.2014.935387

Central Committee of the CPC & State Council. (2011, December 20). Zhongguo nongcun fupin kaifa gangyao (2011–2020 Nian) 中国农村扶贫开发纲要 (2011–2020年) [Outline for Poverty Alleviation and Development in Rural China (2011–2020)]. *Zhonghua Renmin Gongheguo Guowuyuan Gongbao,* (35). https://www.gov.cn/gongbao/content/2011/content_2020905.htm

International Poverty Reduction Centre in China. (2021, March 26). *Quanguo tuopin gongjian kaochadian jianjie: Yunnan Sheng Lancang Xian Menggen Cun Laodabao wenhua fupin xiangmu 全国脱贫攻坚考察点简介:云南省澜沧县勐根村老达保文化扶贫项目* [Introduction to the national poverty alleviation research site: Laodabao Cultural Poverty Alleviation Project in Menggen Village, Lancang County, Yunnan Province]. https://www.iprcc.org.cn/article/42ScDvdWOgc

Li, S. (2022, April 12). *Lancang Xian Laodabao: Nong wen lv ronghe rang "lao dianxing" shu "xin bangyang" 澜沧县老达保:农文旅融合让"老典型"树"新榜样"* [Laodabao in Lancang County: The integration of agriculture, culture and tourism makes the "old typical example" a new role model]. Tencent. https://new.qq.com/rain/a/20220412A02F1400

Li, Y. (2022, December 24). *Gesheng piaoguo Laodabao歌声飘过老达保* [The singing drifts past Laodabao]. Zhongguo Minzu Zongjiao Wang. http://www.mzb.com.cn/html/report/22122358-1.htm

National Bureau of Statistics of China. (2022). *Sanci chanye huafen guiding三次产业划分规定* [Regulations on the three sectors of industries]. http://www.stats.gov.cn/sj/tjbz/gjtjbz/202302/t20230213_1902749.html

National Ethnic Affairs Commission of the People's Republic of China. (n.d.). *Lahu Zu gaikuang 拉祜族概况* [An overview of Lahu ethnic group]. https://www.neac.gov.cn/seac/ztzl/lhz/gk.shtml

State Council Poverty Alleviation and Development Leading Group Office and Editorial Committee of Poverty Alleviation Series Books (Eds.) (2020) Poverty Eradication Awards for Organizational Innovation Pioneers (2018–2020)《脱贫攻坚先锋组织创新奖先进单位事迹 (2018–2020)》, Beijing: China Personnel Publishing House and China Labour and Social Security Publishing Housing.

Wen, Y., Zhang, W., & Wang, Q. (2020). Menggen Cun diyi shuji Hu Hong: Tuoqi fupin mengxiang de "qianlang" 勐根村第一书记胡红:托起扶贫梦想的"前浪" [Hu Hong, the First Secretary of Menggen Village: The "front wave" that supports the dream of poverty alleviation]. *Zhongguo Kexueyuan Yuankan* [Bulletin of Chinese Academy of Sciences], *35*(Z2), 145–148. http://old2022.bulletin.cas.cn/publish_article/2020/Z2/2020S222.htm

Yang, W. (2020). *Lahu Zu cunzhai Laodabao: Xingfu de shenghuo chang chulai 拉祜族村寨老达保:幸福的生活唱出来* [Laodabao, a Lahu village: Sing out a happy life]. Liangmeng Zhongguo. http://union.china.com.cn/txt/2020-08/10/content_41251236.html

Zhang, Y. (2021, August 14). Quanguo Xianjin Jiceng Dangzuzhi Lancang Xian Jiujing Ziang Menggen Cun Laodabao Dang zhibu: Dangyuan daitou cu tuopin, "changge tiaowu" zhu zengshou 全国先进基层党组织 澜沧县酒井乡勐根村老达保党支部: 党员带头促脱贫 "唱歌跳舞"助增收 [National advanced Grassroots Party Organization: Lao Dabao Party Branch, Menggen Village, Jiujing Township, Lancang County: Party members take the lead in promoting poverty alleviation, and "singing and dancing" helps increase income]. Yunnan Wang. https://m.yunnan.cn/system/2021/08/14/031612047.shtml

Zuo, B. & Wen, F. (2017). Cultural identity of contemporary Chinese people. *Bulletin of Chinese Academy of Sciences, 32*(2), 175–187. https://bulletinofcas.researchcommons.org/journal/vol32/iss2/8/

Atuleer Village—The Cliff Village

Despite the rapid growth of economic globalization and internet penetration, poverty remains a pressing issue in the world. There have been notable successful cases of poverty alleviation, particularly in China. One noteworthy case of poverty alleviation in China is Atuleer Village, located in the mountainous region of Sichuan Province. Atuleer Village gained international attention for its unique geographic isolation and challenging living conditions. Situated atop a steep cliff, the village was cut off from the outside world, making accessibility and economic development extremely difficult. Through a comprehensive analysis of the strategies, policies, and interventions implemented in Atuleer Village, this report seeks to provide valuable lessons that can guide future poverty alleviation efforts in China and beyond.

The Focal Issue in China

Despite rapid economic growth in China during the past decades, China encounters severe regional inequality: The gap between the East and West and urban–rural income disparities remained prevalent. Rural areas in Sichuan Province, which is one of China's most populous provinces in the western part, held a higher level of relative poverty. However, agricultural modernization, which is a goal of China's reform and opening up, is always a prerequisite for eventually reaching *xiaokang* society (小康社会, fairly well-off society) and socialism modernization (Hsu 1995; Wong 1998). In addition to capital accumulation in China's coastal regions, the former China's President Hu Jintao also reported at the 18th National Congress of CPC, "China has entered the decisive stage of building a moderately prosperous society in all respects" (Hu 2012). According to the Ministry of Agriculture and Rural Affairs in China, "the key to become fairly well-off is to look at the living

International Poverty Reduction Center In China, *Poverty Alleviation Case Analysis In China*, SpringerBriefs on Case Studies of Sustainable Development,
https://doi.org/10.1007/978-981-97-4537-1_6

standards of villagers" (Han 2013). Hence, dealing with the problem of rural poverty is an indispensable task in China.

In addition, China's goal of poverty alleviation is in line with that of the United Nations, which aims to eradicate poverty worldwide by 2030 (Kenny 2015). Under these circumstances, the targeted poverty alleviation strategy was introduced by China's president Xi Jinping in 2013 (Wang and Ma 2021; Central Institute of Party History and Literature 2018). The case of Atuleer Village, also known as the "Cliff Village", is inevitably a cornerstone of China's poverty alleviation cause (Wang and Ma 2021).

The Focal Village

Atuleer village, which is located at the junction of Zhaojue County, Meigu County, and Leibo County in Sichuan Province, is nestled in a mountainous terrain with an elevation of 800 m (International Poverty Reduction Center in China [IPRCC] 2021). The village is famously referred to as "cliff village" due to its location, which requires villagers to navigate 17 nearly vertical rattan ladders, approximately 100 m long in total and clinging to precipitous cliffs, as the only way to access the outside world. Tragically, there have been many incidents of fatal falls reported along this path (Chen 2020). Within the village, 84 of the 163 registered households (over half) were living below the absolute poverty line of China (Lyu et al. 2020).

The geographical obstacle was the primary cause of poverty in Atuleer village. Consequently, this obstacle gave rise to several key challenges that need to be addressed.

The Key Challenges

The first challenge was the lack of accessible medical and educational services. According to Maslow's hierarchy of needs theory, access to medical and educational services are basic requirements of human basic needs (McLeod 2018). Without the fulfillment of these rights, people are far from "fairly well-off." People in Atuleer village lacked these basic needs because the town was inaccessible. In Atuleer village, educational facilities such as schools atop the cliff were rare. To pursue educational opportunities, students had to go to the center of Zhaojue County. They could not attend preschool and primary education as their counterpart students in urban areas, since they could not climb up and down the horizontal rattan ladder every day (Lyu et al. 2020). Their lack of knowledge restricted their participation in high-value industries, which could lead to intergenerational transmission of poverty. The village had no professional medical services either as receiving medical care was difficult for the elderly and the sick since they lost strength to climb the ladder to the town or county center. Their productivity therefore declined along with their health.

The second key challenge was the underdevelopment of local industries. Due to the geological conditions, the villagers relied mainly on agriculture for their livelihood. Their cultivated crops such as potatoes, corn, and beans from approximately 682 mu of arable land (equivalent to around 450,000 square meters out of the total area of 11,000,000 square meters) (IPRCC 2021). Despite the relatively fertile soil, the lack of modern farming tools and management methods also limited their agricultural productivity. Additionally, the absence of accessible tertiary industries further constrained economic opportunities, resulting in the villagers barely maintaining self-sufficiency (Lyu et al. 2020).

The third key challenge was the isolation and closed management of the village. The geographical barriers severely hindered tourism and external investments (China Current n.d.). Villagers fell victim to closed management, lacking modern facilities such as telecommunications and networks, which significantly limited their employment prospects. Moreover, the absence of external capital inflow prevented the village from developing basic infrastructure such as electricity and concrete roads, impeding its modernization.

The Solutions

Geological constraints are primarily responsible for the low level of development and deep poverty in Atuleer. Building a modern infrastructure and facilities is a major solution. The promotion of agricultural and tourism industries, as well as the relocation of the villagers, further increased the effectiveness of the poverty alleviation program.

The first and foremost solution implemented by the prefecture's government was the construction of steel ladders, which replaced the primitive rattan ladders which were unstable and difficult to use. With funding of CNY 1 million, a new steel-made path which consists of 2,556 steps was constructed in 2016 (IPRCC 2021). It is 2.8 km long and 1.5 m wide. The stable steel ladders remain unmovable in strong winds (Cheng 2020). The time reduction of leaving the village by half an hour proves that the steel ladder highly improves accessibility between the village and the county center (IPRCC 2021).

To further improve the access to educational services, one kindergarten class was set up in the village at the foot of the mountain, and two preschool education sites were set up on the mountain. With the newly constructed schools under the mountain, students can live within the schools walking distance to the schools and reduce the traveling time (Lyu et al. 2020). After preschool, 100% of the school-age children in the "cliff village" can attend school (Lyu et al. 2020).

Also, a clinic near the village at the foot of the mountain had four general practitioners, and a clinic on the mountain ensured that all villagers were cared for in an emergency.

With the support of the stable steel ladders, further construction of other modern infrastructure was less difficult. Hence, concrete road, water pipe, and electric streetlight, and network facilities have been built as well (Luo 2017). One of the ways to deal with closed management is to improve the means of networks and communication. As an advanced productive force, information technology is considered to be an effective means to implement targeted poverty alleviation (Qiang 2022). At the end of 2016, cliff village obtained full coverage of a 4G network, and broadband TV was installed in every household (Luo 2017; Qiang 2022). The introduction of the internet helped villagers communicate with the outside world. With the inflow of more information, the villagers' cognitive model has reversed, and they gradually realized the importance of education to overcome intergenerational poverty (Qiang 2022).

Along with the construction of infrastructure and facilities is the development of businesses. As a result of low productivity in the primitive agriculture sector, the government assigned companies to introduce modern management methods. Xichang Zhongze Company (西昌中泽公司), the national olive growers, was introduced, and Zhaojue Zhi'ermo Olive Industry Development Co., Ltd. (昭觉支尔莫油橄榄产业发展有限公司) were jointly established, with 51% of shares held by Zhongze Company and 49% held by Atuleer village (IPRCC 2021). In addition to growing olives, a professional cooperative was established to plant *Panax notoginseng* (*tianqi* 田七), which covers an area of 12 *mu*. Chinese native plants such as Paris, Chinese ground orchid was also planted, covering an area of nearly 30 mu, with a total investment of nearly CNY 2 million (IPRCC 2021).

With the capital from large companies, the cliff village was able to sign a poverty alleviation e-commerce agreement with JD.com, Inc. (京东) to sell and distribute its "cliff village" brands through e-commerce platforms (IPRCC 2021). By working with the company's equity dividend, land transfer, olive industry base, and e-commerce platform, farmers finally obtained increased income.

Tourism was also an option in the village. By taking advantage of natural features such as canyons, karst caves, hot springs, and so on in the village, local governments provided social funds to establish the cliff village–Guli Grand Canyon scenic area ("悬崖村-古里大峡谷"景区) (IPRCC 2021), and turn cliff village into a national mountain tourism resort, a cultural tourism experience for Yi District (彝区), and an example of using cultural tourism to alleviate poverty.

The growth of the agricultural sector in Atuleer village had a positive impact on the local tourist industry as well. The agricultural products, including peppers, oranges, olives, alpine honey and other crops, plus breeding projects, contributed to sustainable source of income for the villagers (IPRCC 2021). Additionally, various income sources included land transfer, employment, the sale of agricultural products, and profit dividends were explored (IPRCC 2021). Furthermore, the cliff village has attracted about 100,000 tourists annually (IPRCC 2021). The villagers have capitalized on the opportunity by establishing canteens and hotels, as well as selling honey, green peppers, and navel oranges, among other products (IPRCC 2021). As a result, the village earns nearly CNY 1 million annually from tourism, providing a substantial boost to their overall income (IPRCC 2021).

Along with development in the village, the Chinese government also encouraged relocation to improve the living standards of the villagers. The government has constructed 1,400 relocation sites, mainly in Zhaojue County (IPRCC 2021). An example of successful relocation is the villager Mouse Labo (某色拉博) and his family, who now reside in a spacious 100-square-metter county house, a significant improvement from their previous dilapidated mud shelters (TVB Zung Ngai 2021). By May 2020, all 84 registered poverty-stricken households in cliff village had been successfully relocated to other places, allowing the villagers to pursue higher-income jobs in the county (TVB Zung Ngai 2021; Lyu et al. 2020). The measure mainly targets to address the geographical obstacles faced by the villager. While the infrastructure and facilities in cliff village have improved, it is essential to provide the younger (and talented) generation with higher disposable income to unleash their potential (Lyu et al. 2020). As a result, their relocation can create more opportunity for the next generations.

The income of villagers in developing industries increased significantly. The annual per capita income of cliff village has increased from less than CNY 2,000 in 2014 to more than CNY 9,000 in 2020 (IPRCC 2021). Poverty in this village has been eliminated since 2020.

Case Analysis

Economic Development

The success of poverty alleviation in Atuleer village mainly originated from the improvement in capital accumulation, resulting in the growth of the production, and thus raise the full-employment national income, (Wallstreetmojo Team n.d.). Aligning with the Solow Model, when there was continuous technology advancement that drove up production, the whole output curve shifted upward as the marginal productivity of capital and labor increased.

However, capital in Atuleer village was difficult to accumulate due to its geographical constraints. These factors inhibited investment, tourism, and infrastructure construction. Considering this, the local government first dealt with the root problem of the geological constraints in Atuleer village. Construction of the steel ladder, which greatly increased accessibility between the village and the county (Lyu et al. 2020), provided a core foundation for further development due to the ease of accumulating capital and productivity boost.

Moreover, due to the effective investment, farmers were able to diversify their income. The investment of agricultural enterprises not only provided farmers with an opportunity to grow economics crops, but also allowed them to offer the indigenous crops to attract tourists. Different featured business had emerged, such as cultural tourism and key opinion leader (KOL, also known as social media influencer) economy. In addition, *Yi* Embroidery workshop (彝绣工坊) was established in the resettlement site, and training for chefs was also arranged (Wu 2022). These kinds of development laid a solid foundation for income growth of local peasants, and this effectively kept villagers from returning to poverty without the support of society and the government.

In the long run, production had increased. Investment in education, accompanied by the children's ability to attend school, proved to be effective in increasing innovative ideas and marginal productivity of capital and labor (Wolla and Sullivan 2017). Medical investment could also increase human capital, which is positively and tightly related to people's income (World Bank 2018). In addition to educational and medical services, the interest-sharing mechanism triggered the incentive to produce as well when Xichang Zhongze Company collaborated with Atuleer village to develop modern management methods and an innovative planting industry.

Sustainable Development

Of the UN 17 Sustainable Development Goals (SDGs), "no poverty" is Goal 1 (United Nations 2022). Eliminating poverty, which aims to "end poverty in all its forms everywhere" (United Nations 2022), is indispensable to Atuleer village in conjunction with Goal 3, "good health and well-being," Goal 4, "quality education," and Goal 9, "industry, innovation, and infrastructure." The development has also balanced economic growth and cultural conservation, which has fulfilled both Goal 8, "decent work and economic growth" and Goal 11, "sustainable cities and communities." Eliminating poverty in Atuleer village is related to Goal 10, "reduced inequalities," which is crucial for China's social stability and sustainable development. The Chinese government's success in poverty alleviation enhances the progress of UN SDGs in the area.

Reaching Goal 9 during the process of poverty alleviation was a resounding success. As discussed in the case analysis section, investment in infrastructure and industry development were the keyways for Atuleer village to eliminate poverty. The construction of the steel ladders, which replaced the dangerous and primitive rattan ladders, highly increases the accessibility of the villages to the outside world. This not only help villagers gain education and medical services in town, but also provided an opportunity for further state investment in a modern infrastructure, such as network, concrete roads, etc. In addition, the introduction of Zhaojue Zhi'ermo Olive Industry Development Co. Ltd., supported industry in the village. Farmers could capitalize on modern management methods in the agricultural industry and export the output through the development. Hence, the process of poverty alleviation achieved Goal 9.

In the long term, improvements in education and medical services are two strategies to alleviate poverty in Atuleer village, which also achieve Goals 3 and 4. Education is a powerful contributor to future economic development and facilitates health and hygiene. This eventually ensures social mobility and stability. In addition to infrastructure development to reduce students' commuting time and difficulties in attending schools, the relocation of some villagers made it easier for them to enjoy higher-quality education in town. The annual subsidy standard for each student is CNY 4,500 (Huang 2020).

In addition, the steel ladders tend to be more stable than the rattan ladders, which directly guarantees villagers' health and safety. As a result, the goal of good health and well-being is developing steadily.

The development here does not destroy the cultural heritage. Instead, it could achieve SDG 11: "Sustainable cities and communities" and SDG 8: "Decent work and economic growth" at the same time. Although some villagers relocated, 30 households decided to stay in the original village. In the future, the Atuleer village will also be developed into a traditional cultural site for preservation, and the remaining villagers will become guardians of the local culture, showing the historical fragments of Yi culture to the visitors (China Current n.d.; Huang 2020). For example, the *Yi* Embroidery workshop in the resettlement site was established (Wu 2022). This has helped protect and safeguard cultural and natural heritage, while it has also promoted tourism and economic growth.

Furthermore, the vision is to alleviate the long-existing district disparities in China. Regional disparity, especially the disparity between the East and West region has been major regional inequality problems. People's living standards in China's western rural regions are generally lower than those of the coastal cities. From global experience, such development inequality could undermine social cohesion among the regions, increasing political and social tensions and, in some circumstances, driving instability and conflicts (Floerkemeier et al. 2021). Worse still, since the ethnic minorities are mainly concentrated in the Western China, such as Yunnan, Sichuan, Tibet, Xinjiang, the imbalanced development may trigger ethnic conflicts, which could have a detrimental impact on national security. Since minority groups are more likely to live in remote districts, which is reflected in this case study, they are the main benefactor of the government's poverty alleviation project.

In the case of cliff village, poverty prevailed due to geographical barriers, which stifled the potential development of the villagers in education, medical, and other job opportunities. However, similar problems have occurred less frequently since the initiation of the poverty alleviation project. The promotion of tourism and the improvement of transportation have achieved considerable success. With the inflow of tourists, villagers started individual agricultural businesses and, as tour guides, have successfully sustained their daily lives. It is estimated that the per capita income of the poor population in cliff village reached more than CNY 9,000 in 2020, nearly five times of that in 2014 (IPRCC 2021). All the villagers are no longer belong to poverty. Thus, the government's efforts in poverty alleviation facilitate the progress of the SDGs in combating poverty and improving the living standard of the villagers.

To conclude, the poverty alleviation project could significantly reduce the poverty rate and improve the villagers' standard of living, which can be considered as progress toward the SDGs. Meanwhile, the improvement of transportation and the upgrade in education level has reduced the possibility of returning to poverty. In general, the project is progressive and preserves human dignity and well-being and enhances human rights inside China's territory.

Best Practice Case Reference: Xiadang Village, at Ningde, Fujian Province—Multidisciplinary Poverty Reduction Strategy

In poverty-stricken villages, such as Xiadang village (下党村) in Ningde, Fujian Province, the poverty alleviation measures through infrastructure construction, business development, agricultural support, and tourism promotion have proved effective (Chen et al. 2018).

In the 1990s, Xiadang was a poverty-stricken township at the provincial level, one of four in Ningde region and the only "five no villages" in the province: no roads, no tap water, no electric lighting, no financial revenue, and no government office (Chen et al. 2018). The per capita annual income was less than CNY 200 (Chen et al. 2018). The mountainous area means that people have to climb mountains when entering and leaving the village, which makes it difficult for local villagers to access medical services, pick up fertilizer, and raise pigs (Chen et al. 2018).

After research, the government accumulated CNY 720,000 to support the infrastructure construction of the Xiadang village. It is mainly used for water, electricity, lighting, highway construction, and office space (Chen et al. 2018). Xiadang villagers were also enabled to develop tea industry and sell the production out ofvillages. Other handmade local specialties sold in the teahouse also increases their disposable income (Chen et al. 2018). At present, most of the households in Xiadang village have an annual income of more than CNY 20,000 (Chen et al. 2018).

International Comparative Studies

The Chinese government and those of other countries have taken measures to alleviate poverty. Nepal, a landlocked country in South Asia, is mainly situated in the Himalayas (National Planning Commission 2021), and encountered a similar problem as Cliff village in Liangshan, Sichuan, China.

The inaccessibility of the country due to the mountainous regions and the lack of transportation links, in conjunction with underinvestment in educational and medical services, resulted in it becoming one of the poorest countries (Hong 2022). In a measure like the poverty alleviation method in Atuleer village, the government of Nepal improved infrastructure such as concrete roads and network facilities for better accessibility, which not only enabled local residents gain access to medical and education services, but also attracts some foreign direct investment (Chhetry 2004; Hong 2022). At the same time, it implemented several policies to develop the agricultural sector, such as land reform (Chhetry 2004; Hong 2022).

After capital accumulation, its poverty alleviation measures showed some signs of effectiveness, such that between 2014 and 2019, Nepal reduced its poverty from 30.1% to 17.4% (National Planning Commission 2021). However, the economic growth of Nepal cannot cover the heavy debt from foreign countries, which causes some uncertainty in its economic sustainability (Hong 2022). There are several reasons for this. In Nepal, the government put much focus on agricultural development, while the arable land suitable for farming in this agricultural country only accounts for 20% of its national territory (Hong 2022). Notwithstanding the improvement of transportation links, the travel accessibility is still low, which cannot completely boost investor confidence.

The case of Atuleer village, in which the key challenges and solutions were similar, could be a reference to Nepal. Rather than solely relying on capital accumulation in Atuleer village, China tried to diversify the income of villagers. The Nepal government might thus consider taking the advantage of its scenic spot in the Himalayas and invest more in tourism to diversify people's income. This could lead to more sustainable economic growth and improve people's living standard.

Key Learnings

The case of poverty alleviation in Atuleer village fulfils the following SDGs: Goal 1. No poverty; Goal 3. Good health and well-being; Goal 4. Quality education; Goal 8. Decent work and economic growth; Goal 9. Industry, innovation, and infrastructure; Goal 10. Reduced inequalities; and Goal 11. Sustainable cities and communities.

To summarize, the key learning points from this case are: first, Poverty alleviation measures shall cater local conditions; second, Infrastructure construction and investment, which increases capital accumulation, are usually the first steps of poverty alleviation; third, Improvements in education and medical services are required for long-term development, and fourth, Relocation is an option to deal with geological constraints.

References

Central Institute of Party History and Literature (Ed.). (2018). *Xi Jinping fupin lunshu zhaibian 习近平扶贫论述摘编* [Eradicating Poverty] (1st ed.). Central Party Literature Press. https://www.12371.cn/special/xxzd/dzs/18/

Chen, J. (2020). Si nian jiu tan "Xuanya Cun", cong tanqi dao jianshe xing 四年九探"悬崖村"从探奇到建设性 [Nine explorations of cliff village in four years: From exploring to being constructive]. *The Chinese Journalist* (11), 60–61. https://bit.ly/43MXXEf

Chen, M., Wang, Z., & Lin, W. (2018, February 17). Fujian Ningde Xiadang Xiang: Zong Shuji zhiyin de "xingfu lu" yue zou yue kuanguang 福建宁德下党乡:总书记指引的"幸福路"越走越宽广 [Xiadang village in Ningde, Fujian: The "Happiness Road" guided by the General Secretary is wider and wider]. *People Daily*. http://politics.people.com.cn/n1/2018/0217/c1001-29825407.html

Cheng, S. (2020, October 28). 'Cliff village' in SW China's Sichuan shakes off poverty. *People's Daily*. http://en.people.cn/n3/2020/1028/c90000-9773815.html

Chhetry, D. (2004). Practices of poverty measurement and poverty profile of Nepal. *Asian Development Bank*. https://www.adb.org/publications/practices-poverty-measurement-and-poverty-profile-nepal

China Current. (n.d.). *Xuanya Cun 懸崖村* [Cliff village]. Retrieved September 27, 2022, from https://chinacurrent.com/education/article/2021/06/22181.html

Floerkemeier, H., Spatafora, N., & Venables, A. (2021). Regional disparities, growth, and inclusiveness. *IMF Working Papers, 21*(38). https://doi.org/10.5089/9781513569505.001

Han, C. (2013, January 7). Xiaokang bu xiaokang guanjian zai laoxiang小康不小康 关键在老乡 [The key to achieve moderate prosperity is to look at the living standard of villagers]. *People's Daily*. http://cpc.people.com.cn/n/2013/0107/c351153-20116983.html

Hong, X. (2022, June 20). *Nibo'er shi: Cengjing minglie shijie shi da qiongguo, Nibo'er zhengfu caiqu le naxie tuopin cuoshi? 尼泊爾史:曾經名列世界十大窮國,尼泊爾政府採取了哪些脫貧措施?* [History of Nepal: Once ranked among the top ten poor countries in the world, what measures has the Nepalese government taken to alleviate poverty?]. The News Lens. https://www.thenewslens.com/article/168434

Hsu, I. C. Y. (1995). *The rise of modern China* (5th ed.). Oxford University Press.

Hu, J. (2012, November 8). Hu Jintao zai Zhongguo Gongchandang Di Shiba Ci Quanguo Daibiao Dahui shang de baogao 胡锦涛在中国共产党第十八次全国代表大会上的报告 [Hu Jintao's report at the 18th National Congress of the Chinese Communist Party]. *People's Daily Online*. http://cpc.people.com.cn/n/2012/1118/c64094-19612151.html

Huang, Z. (2020, May 12). Residents in cliff-top village moving to new urban homes. *China Daily*. https://global.chinadaily.com.cn/a/202005/12/WS5eb9fda5a310a8b241154f24_2.html

International Poverty Reduction Center in China. (2021, March 22). *Quanguo tuopin gongjian kaocha dian jianjie: Sichuan Sheng Liangshan Zhou Zhaojue Xian Atulie'er Cun 全国脱贫攻坚考察点简介:四川省凉山州昭觉县阿土列尔村* [Introduction to the national poverty alleviation investigation site: Atuleer Vvillage, Zhaojue County, Liangshan Prefecture, Sichuan Province]. https://www.iprcc.org.cn/article/42PQjSWmp88

Kenny, C. (2015, April). *Goal 1: End poverty in all its forms everywhere*. United Nations. https://www.un.org/en/chronicle/article/goal-1-end-poverty-all-its-forms-everywhere#:~:text=The%20first%20target%20of%20the

Luo, Y. (2017). Liangshan Dianxin kaitong "Xuanya Cun" youxian wuxian wangluo ji yewu 凉山电信开通"悬崖村"有线无线网络及业务 [Liangshan Telecom opens wired and wireless network and business in 'cliff village']. *Communication & Information Technology, 1*(30).

Lyu, Q., Wu, G., & Wang, D. (2020, May 14). China focus: Relocated villagers leave poverty on clifftop. *Xinhua Net*. http://www.xinhuanet.com/english/2020-05/14/c_139056868.htm

McLeod, S. A. (2018, May 21). *Maslow's hierarchy of needs*. Retrieved from https://www.simplypsychology.org/maslow.html

National Planning Commission. (2021). *Nepal multidimensional poverty index 2021: Analysis towards action*. Government of Nepal. https://www.unicef.org/nepal/media/14346/file/MPI_Report_2021.pdf

Qiang, Y. (2022, June 1). *Cong Xuanya Cun "tibian" kan jingzhun tuopin 从悬崖村"梯变"看精准脱贫* [Targeted Poverty Alleviation from the 'Ladder Change' of cliff village]. Gongchandang Yuan Wang. https://tougao.12371.cn/gaojian.php?tid=3377605

TVB Zung Ngai [TVB Variety]. (2021, August 30). *Mou kung zi lou – Zoi gin jyun ngaai cyun! Jan leoi si soeng zeoi daai jing jik dei bun cin - Tyut pan 無窮之路 – 再見懸崖村!人類史上最大型易地搬遷 - 脫貧* [Infinite Road - Goodbye cliff village! The largest relocation in human history - Poverty alleviation] [Video]. YouTube. https://www.youtube.com/watch?v=q4mQHP3L9M4

United Nations (2022). The Sustainable Development Goals Report 2022 (pp. 26–27). https://unstats.un.org/sdgs/report/2022/

Wallstreetmojo Team. (n.d.). Solow Growth Model. *WallStreetMojo*. Retrieved December 29, 2022, from https://www.wallstreetmojo.com/solow-growth-model/

Wang, X. & Ma, X. (2021, May 2). Gaobie shidai pinkun, Liangshan jubian de beihou 告别世代贫困 凉山巨变的背后 [Farewell to Generation Poverty Behind the Great Changes in Liangshan]. *China Youth Daily*. http://m.cyol.com/gb/articles/2021-05/02/content_b8eejfLyJ.html

Wolla, S. A. & Sullivan, J. (2017, January). Education, income, and wealth. *Economic Research—St. Louis Fed*. https://research.stlouisfed.org/publications/page1-econ/2017/01/03/education-income-and-wealth#:~:text=The%20relationship%20between%20education%20and

Wong, J. (1998). Xiao-kang: Deng Xiaoping's socio-economic development target for China. *Journal of Contemporary China, 7*(17), 141–152. https://doi.org/10.1080/10670569808724309

World Bank. (2018, December 7). *Lack of health care is a waste of human capital: 5 Ways to achieve universal health coverage by 2030.* https://www.worldbank.org/en/news/immersive-story/2018/12/07/lack-of-health-care-is-a-waste-of-human-capital-5-ways-to-achieve-universal-health-coverage-by-2030

Wu, G. (2022, March 11). *Tuopin hou de "Xuanya Cun" jiu zheyang chengwei ling ren xiangwang de "shi he yuanfang" 脱贫后的"悬崖村"就这样成为令人向往的"诗和远方"* [The "cliff village" after poverty alleviation has thus become a yearning "poem and distance"]. Jiemian Xinwen. https://www.jiemian.com/article/7196642.html

Hunan Orphan-Support Program

Children, especially orphans, are among the most vulnerable groups of society, and poverty among orphans has long been a major challenge in China. According to the latest national report, by the end of 2021, China had 173,000 registered orphans; among them, 53,000 were living in welfare institutions (Ministry of Civil Affairs 2021). Although the living standards and educational level of these nationally supported orphans have been steadily rising over the years, it is still hard for those working-age orphans to gain financial independence and overcome poverty. Thus, most of them constantly depend on governmental subsidies for basic living needs, even in their adulthood period (Shang and Li 2015). Consequently, orphans' dependence on welfare system has become a heavy burden of local governments and a major challenge in poverty alleviation.

Academic sphere has made various policy suggestions, and one of the common recommendations is to provide vocational education to develop orphans' employability. However, several previous vocational education projects have shown little effect. Orphans are found to have both academic and emotional difficulties in completing ordinary vocational education, and many still cannot or even do not want to find a self-sufficient job after graduation (Yuan et al. 2018). Therefore, emotional support and development guidance are also needed for such projects to be implemented. This case demonstrates the innovative approach adopted by the Hunan Architecture Senior Technical School in its project to help Xiangxi (湘西) orphans. They combined vocational education, a placement scheme, and emotional support and development guidance to maximize orphans' employability. Background information and a comparison with other similar international cases are provided here for reference.

International Poverty Reduction Center In China, *Poverty Alleviation Case Analysis In China*, SpringerBriefs on Case Studies of Sustainable Development,
https://doi.org/10.1007/978-981-97-4537-1_7

Orphan Poverty in China

This section discusses the major issues of orphan poverty in China and related national policies.

Major Issues

Currently, orphans in China generally live under a satisfactory level of material support, around CNY 1257.2 per person per month, comparing with CNY 711.4 of minimum living security for urban residents (Ministry of Civil Affairs 2021). Meanwhile, young orphans receive free compulsory education, which covers primary school and junior high school. Moreover, for orphans with physical or mental disabilities, there have also been systemic mechanisms for their lifelong support. Therefore, the main issues have shifted to developmental support for working-age orphans.

Lack of Effective Welfare Withdrawal Mechanism. In China, government-supported orphans mainly live in child welfare institutions (儿童福利院), which were designed in the planned economy period to support orphans' living, medical care, and education until they were provided with jobs in some state-owned companies. In this ideal framework, welfare support terminates at the time of employment which would grant orphans financial independence. However, with the rise of a market economy and collapse of numerous state-owned firms, obtaining employment is getting progressively more difficult for adult orphans. Thus, an increasing number of older and even adult orphans are stuck in welfare institutes. Although orphans would have stopped receiving living allowance once they were older than 18 and have completed education, in practice, most welfare institutions could not completely withdraw financial support and have maintained free accommodations for adult orphans (Shang and Li 2015). Estimates indicate that currently at least 20% of government supported orphans are over 16, and every year more than 10,000 orphans grow to adulthood (Shang 2008). Their dependence has become a heavy burden for the welfare system and will ultimately deteriorate the quality of orphan support in China.

Lack of Systematic Higher Vocational Education and Career Support. Currently, orphans' systematic education support ends at junior high school. For senior high school and above, which includes senior high school, university, and their corresponding levels of vocational education, orphans can still receive financial support, yet enrollment standards only slightly decrease comparing with ordinary students (Yuan et al. 2018). Although orphans' academic performance is inferior to that of ordinary students, vocational schools generally do not have targeted education plans for them, often leading to decreased quality of vocational education and increased dropout rates (Chen 2019). Consequently, a large portion of older orphans cannot receive or complete higher vocational education, which significantly weakens their employability. Employment is also hard for those graduated due to their lack of job-seeking skills and connections. Although many vocational schools have a job allocation mechanism for graduates, as most orphans are unclear about their career path and have done little career planning, they still experience low employment and job retention (Yuan et al. 2018). These all contribute to older orphans' financial dependence.

Lack of Emotional Support. Compared with ordinary vocational education students, orphans usually require more emotional support; a lack of such resources can cause lower education quality and graduation rates. Psychologically, orphans generally experience both learning anxiety and social anxiety, since their previous education was generally completed in welfare institutes which are of inferior quality and less socially connected comparing to ordinary schools (Yuan et al. 2018). However, as orphans need to receive higher vocational education outside welfare institutes, they often cannot find trustworthy individuals with whom to share their troubles and thoughts. These troubles would turn into psychological disorders, such as autism, severe self-doubt, or even antisocial personalities (Zhang et al. 2009; Yuan et al. 2018), which can cause further social problems.

National Policies

To address these issues, state-level policies have been implemented:

Skill-Based Poverty Alleviation Thousand Schools Action. This policy aimed to provide, by 2020, free vocational education and an employment scheme for any orphan students from poor families. Under this policy, for the first time, older orphans were principally guaranteed higher vocational education (Ministry of Human Resources and Social Security & Poverty Alleviation Office 2016).

Implementation Opinions on Deeply Promoting the Skill-Based Poverty Alleviation Thousand Schools Action. This policy was an extension of the 2016 version. It further established high-quality vocational schools as key actors in skill-based poverty alleviation. In the context of this policy, vocational schools with good teaching quality and a high employment rate would be selected to provide free education for financially distressed students. Moreover, such schools were required to establish a point-to-point relationship with poor areas to ensure every qualified child benefited from the policy (Ministry of Human Resources and Social Security & Poverty Alleviation Office 2019).

Background

This section introduces the background information about the district and institutions involved in the case. The higher vocational education system of mainland China is also introduced.

Xiangxi

Xiangxi, or Xiangxi Tujia and Miao Autonomous Prefecture (湘西土家族苗族自治州), is a northeast district of Hunan Province. According to the latest provincial statistic, Xiangxi is the poorest district in the area (Hunan Provincial Bureau of Statistics & Survey Office 2021). Xiangxi had 2,180 legally identified orphans and 3,270 whose parents are missing or cannot provide support nor care. Those orphans mainly lived with grandparents or in welfare institutions.

Xiangxi Love Park

Established in 2015, Xiangxi Love Park is the first orphan welfare institution in the Xiangxi autonomous prefecture, Hunan Province and hosts roughly 150 orphans (Mo 2021). The Love Park provides accommodation and education from primary to junior high level to young orphans, and is renowned for its detailed emotional support. This institution has collaborated with various high schools, including both ordinary high schools and higher vocational education institutions. These are expected to provide diversified education channels for orphans.

The Love Park partnered with Hunan Architecture Senior Technical School in 2017. Starting in 2018, orphan students aged 13–15 who had completed junior high school but failed to be admitted to ordinary senior high schools were selected for the case project annually.

Hunan Architecture Senior Technical School

Being located in Changsha, Hunan Architecture Senior Technical School is a national vocational school and a recognized vocational education institute with a graduate employment rate exceeding 98% (Hunan Architecture Senior Technical School n.d.). Its primary focus is providing architecture and construction-related vocational education to students holding junior or senior high school diplomas.

The school was founded by Hunan Construction Engineering Group (湖南建工集团) and maintains a close collaboration with the group regarding the placement of its graduates. It is recognized as a listed institution under the Action of Thousand Schools (千校行动) policy.

In the case project, orphans received their higher vocational education in the school. Since 2017, the project has received five groups of orphans, and each group had around 10 students, and the first three groups graduated by 2022 (Fig. 1).

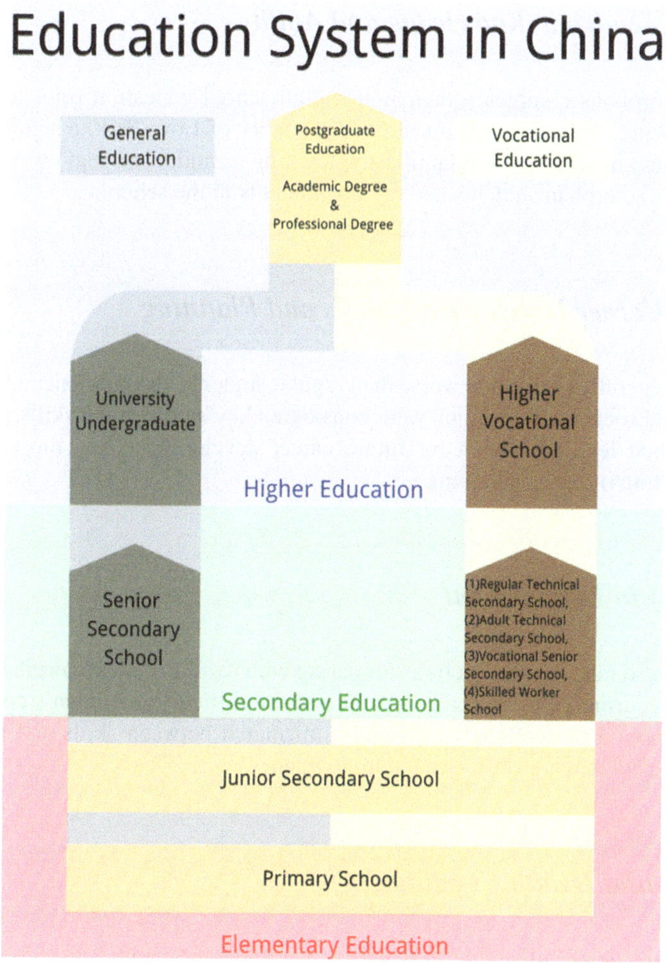

Fig. 1 Education system in Mainland China. *Note* From report on the development of vocational education in China 2012–2022, Ministry of Education of the People's Republic of China (2022)

The Key Challenges

This section further expands on the major issues of older-orphan development in specific points by referring to the case context.

Inferior Academic Knowledge and Ability

Although orphans completed their junior high school education prior to the case project, owing to the limited education and quality of Love Park, a significant gap in academic knowledge, skill familiarity, learning attitude, and logic was observed between these orphan students and regular students in the school.

Lack of Career Development Skills and Planning

Orphans generally performed worse than regular students in communication, collaboration, and socialization, which were considered key employment skills. They also demonstrated less motivation for future career development, and most had little understanding of career planning.

Difficulty in Employment

As mentioned in the earlier section comparing with regular students, orphan students find that securing their first employment is more difficult. In Hunan's context, the lack of targeted professional skills and a mismatch between skills and jobs were identified as two major obstacles to employment.

Poor Mental Health Condition

Orphans are more vulnerable to negative emotions and mental disorders. For the orphans in this case, loneliness and low self-esteem were the two most observed psychological issues. Compounded by the heavy learning burden, unfamiliar environment, and volatile emotional changes of teenagers, these mental health issues can develop into severe problems.

Solution

The project was based on the collaboration of Love Park, the school, and companies in the architecture industry. (Fig. 2) Love Park was the source of the orphans, the school was the platform for vocational education, and the industry provided employments for orphans after their graduation. Four strategies in this project can be generalized: (a) financial support, (b) skill development and employment support, (c) mentor scheme, and (d) mental support. While the school was the main platform and facilitator for solutions, Love Park and companies also contributed to these solutions.

Financial Support

All orphan students were exempt from tuition fees, and other living fees were charged with discounted price. The school provided allowance for transportation and other possible expenses. Scholarships were also established to reward students with excellent academic performance. Moreover, orphans continued to receive a monthly living allowance from Love Park.

Skill Development and Employment Support

Orphan students were allowed to choose any profession from the school curriculum based on their interests (Liu et al. 2018). Each profession was associated with a position in a partner company. The teaching content and assessment of the profession were tailored to the specific requirements of the jobs to ensure orphan students to be equipped with all necessary skills after education. Moreover, field trips and internships at the partner companies were organized to further strengthen students' professional ability. After graduation, orphan students were immediately allocated

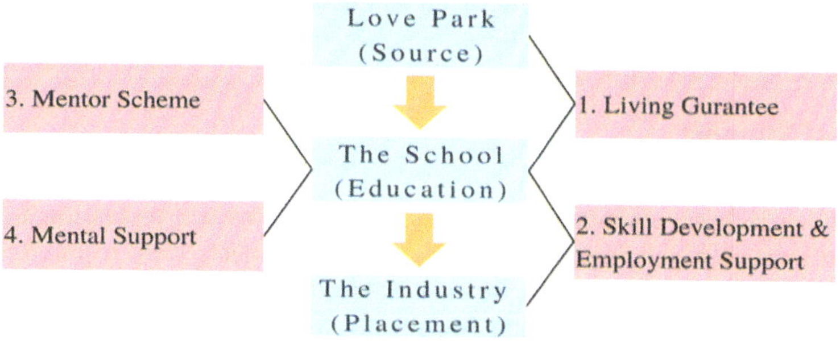

Fig. 2 Role of Love Park, school, and industry in the orphans' support and development

to the job positions associated with their profession. Additional onboard training for specific tools or employment skills were also provided by the school and the partner companies, if needed.

In addition to this targeted placement scheme, the school also provided references and further training to students who wished to change jobs. Starting in 2020, orphan students were also encouraged to take college entrance exams (大专单招考试) for further vocational education (Huang 2021).

Mentor Scheme

To provide comprehensive support to each orphan, a mentorship program was implemented, focusing on the following key areas (Huang 2021):

Academic Tutor. Each orphan was assigned one tutor, who was usually a well-known and experienced teacher at the school, to guide their professional study. The tutors helped the orphan student to follow the course content and to improve their learning ability. Additional guidance was provided if the orphan students were to prepare for skill competitions or qualification exams.

Partner Family. Each orphan was partnered with a teaching staff's family to fulfill their emotional needs. The family generally treated the orphan as their own member and conducted activities such as celebrating the orphan's birthday, spending time together during traditional festivals and school holidays, and providing illness care (Liu et al. 2018). Moreover, the partner family was also able to provide employment resources for their associated orphan student.

Development Mentor. Each orphan was paired with a member of the Communist Party of China (CPC) who served as their development mentor. These mentors played a crucial role in guiding the orphan students' career and life planning. Regular communication between mentors and orphans facilitated guidance in making informed choices regarding their personal and professional growth. Orphan students were encouraged to explore various professions, participate in skill competitions and qualification exams, and set ambitious yet attainable life goals (Chen 2020).

Mental Support

In addition to basic emotional care, the school also provided professional mental support through psychological counseling. Orphan students were required to take regular overall psychological assessments, and results were filed for each student for continuous tracking and monitoring. Meanwhile, the counseling room also provided orphan students with mental health education classes and regular psychological chats in both one-to-one and group forms.

Outcomes and Analysis

The effectiveness of the case project is analyzed in this section, taking into account the identified major problems and specific challenges.

Quality of Vocational Education

The orphan students showed significant average improvement in their academic performance as a result of the project. In the first two semesters, there was an approximate 30% increase of exam scores. In skill acquisition, they had also acquired essential skills in sketching and computer modeling, starting from scratch. From the employment results of these students, their professional ability has also been recognized by the architecture industry. Individually, some of the orphan students achieved extraordinary professional results. For example, one student from the 2017 cohort passed provincial selection and was able to represent Hunan Province in a national skill competition (Chen 2020). Some other students, especially those in 2020 and later cohorts, were able to continue with their vocational education in colleges (大专) after admission through entrance exams (Hunan Architecture Senior Technical School 2020a).

The overall and individual performances of the orphan students demonstrate the high quality of vocational education. Considering the significant initial gap between the orphan students and ordinary students, the achieved results should be considered as meeting the education goal of the SDGs and reducing inequalities. The vocational education provided to the orphan students was able to bridge the gap with ordinary students and equip them with skills and knowledge for their career.

Employment and Further Development

Overall, 100% employment was achieved for project students. Although this was one part of the project design, the employment rate was still high for these orphan students after considering longer time horizons. As the students were allocated to positions which highly related to their education, improved job satisfaction was also observed. Individually, some excellent students were able to explore more options after their graduation. As mentioned earlier, some students were able to pursue further vocational education, while others, after leaving their allocated jobs, achieved independent employment in their careers ranging from junior engineer in major state-owned firms to logistics positions in the military (Hunan Architecture Senior Technical School 2020b).

Considering that most of the mentioned jobs provided salaries which could support a "*xiaokang*-oriented," i.e., fairly well-off, livelihood, these orphan students can be regarded as having escaped from absolute poverty and achieved their financial independence. More importantly, such financial independence enabled these orphan students to support their grandparents and other economically disadvantaged relatives. The case project impart aligns with the concept of "One person gets trained; one person gets employed; then the whole family gets rescued" (培训一个，就业一人，脱贫一家) and "developmental poverty alleviation" (造血式扶贫), as it profoundly improved the quality of life of individual orphans and their families and relatives. Therefore, the UN's goals of No-poverty and Decent work were achieved. Furthermore, the close collaboration between welfare institutions, the school, and industry companies demonstrated in the case also contributes to achieving SDG goal 17, which emphasizes the importance of partnerships for sustainable development.

Mental Condition

During the orphans' study in the school, results from Mental Health Questionnaires (UPI), Students' Symptom Checklist 90 (SCL-90), and Satisfaction with Life Scale all showed improved psychological condition. Also, there were no dropouts in any cohort of the case project. Individually, some students described themselves as "more motivated to work" or "more socialized" after graduation. Although follow-on mental assessments for students who have graduated are not available, at least their mental issues were successfully tackled during their study in the school, which is still progress considering the prevalence of mental problems in previous similar projects. Hence, the case project achieved the SDG goal of good health and well-being.

Further Impact on Society

Considering the small scale of the case project (approximately 10 students per year; only open to orphans from Xiangxi Love Park), it is difficult to observe the project's immediate impact on Chinese society. Therefore, the project evaluation should focus more on its inspirational impact. Based on the analysis in earlier sections, the project has demonstrated its potential as a feasible solution to the older-orphan problem in contemporary China. As the project has addressed issues in educational equality, employment opportunity equality, and health and medical care equality, it should also be considered as the implementation of the SDG goal of Reduced inequalities.

Best Practice Case Reference: Tianjin Women and Children Development Foundation (天津妇女儿童发展基金会)—"Five Support and One Insurance" (五救助一补助)

(The State Council Leading Group of Poverty Alleviation and Development 2020)

This section presents a similar exemplary poverty alleviation case in Tianjin municipality, comparing with the Hunan case.

Summary of the Practice

The Tianjin Women and Children Development Foundation is a government-run welfare organization in Tianjin, China. The "Five Support and One Insurance" project is a flagship poverty alleviation initiative implemented by organization. The project specifically targets low-income single mothers in the municipality and aim to improve their overall well-being and alleviate poverty.

The project covers five key areas of support, which include living, medical, entrepreneurship, educational, and emotional support. Additionally, the project incorporates health insurance coverage for low-income single mothers in the municipality. The foundation has also extended its projects to conduct similar projects covering the rural seniors, left-behind children, and other vulnerable groups in Tianjin, Jing–Jin–Ji Metropolitan Region (京津冀城市群), an economic region surrounding the municipalities of Beijing and Tianjin, and the Western China. Those projects have also achieved much success so far.

Relevant Learning Points from the Practice

While the above-mentioned practice has generated various inspiring examples of different aspects, such as innovative insurance products for vulnerable minorities. This section mainly focuses on the learning points from educational, business, and emotional perspectives.

Educational Support: Pair Help

In the educational support program, single-mother families form pairs with NGOs or charity enterprises, which support children's education from single-parent families both materially and mentally. The program has helped more than 1,000 students from single-parent families to receive tertiary education.

Entrepreneurship Support: Enterprise Fund

An enterprise fund was created to grant interest-free loans for low-income single mothers to start their own business. Further enterprise guidance is also provided to help them expand the business. Several female-owned enterprises have emerged from this program.

Emotional Support: Fortitude Mother Club

Emotional support was highly emphasized by the foundation as a key component of the project. Fortitude Mother Club (坚强母亲俱乐部) was organized. This club serves as a mutual support platform for single-parent families to seek psychological assistance.

The foundation also recognized role models in poverty reduction to boost motivation and morale. Furthermore, professional psychological consulting organizations were invited to offer mental health support and treatment to families in need.

Comparison

Both the Tianjin case and the Hunan case have emphasized educational, employment/entrepreneurship, and emotional support. While the Hunan case had more institutional planning, the Tianjin case emphasized more stimulating mutual help and social support. The difference may be caused by differences in the target groups, as orphans are likely to be less independent and self-motivated than single mothers. Both cases have provided a glimpse into the practice of developmental poverty alleviation in contemporary China.

International Comparative Studies

Currently, related international projects can be divided into two categories, child poverty alleviation and higher education financial support. Each category contains numerous projects conducted in different regions of the world, while only a few projects have combined the two perspectives.

Projects on Children Poverty Alleviation

Based on the authors' best knowledge, most major international charity groups and NGOs, such as Save the Children, have only general child poverty alleviation initiatives. Typical focus of these projects is on basic living conditions such as sufficient food and clean water. While many projects have also tried to address education, their efforts are mostly on literacy and numeracy improvement, which is roughly equivalent to primary or junior high school education. There is little discussion about the development of older children.

Projects on Higher Education Financial Support

Such supports are often provided by locally based foundations or educational institutes themselves. Typically, those projects offer scholarships for students from poor families to support their further education. While scholarships have been diversified to cover all possible higher education options, the number of scholarships is often limited comparing with educational costs. Furthermore, there are no guarantees of general education after junior high school or arrangements for employments after the graduation.

Combination: Lack of International Counterpart

Overall, few projects are able to provide higher vocational education support to older orphans. The situation is understandable, since in many developing countries, basic living and elementary education are still unsolved problems. However, current educational support for orphans, or for poor children in general, in those countries may be insufficient for them to ultimately achieve financial independence and get rid of poverty. Higher vocational education is needed for complete poverty alleviation projects, and the design of the case project could offer some good references.

Despite the lack of similar international cases, an interesting project is found in Kenya (Skovdal et al. 2011). In that project, orphan relief was integrated into the community alleviation movement, which was carried out according to plans made by local residents. According to development plans, residents were trained in skills and provided with resources for implementation. One of these plans was about care and education of orphans. The whole process resembles the menu-based poverty alleviation in China in certain ways, with overall satisfactory outcomes (Skovdal et al. 2011). Such a community self-help project would be an ideal example to many underdeveloped areas and could be used to deliver primary or even junior high school education to orphans.

Related SDGs

SDGs	Case project feature
1. No poverty	Improved life quality for orphans and their family
3. Good health and well-being	Improved mental health condition
4. Quality education	Vocational education of high quality
8. Decent work and economic growth	100% employment rate for orphan participants
10. Reduced inequalities	Educational, employment, and medical support for orphans
17. Partnerships for the goal	Close collaboration with local governments and industry

Key Learnings

Importance of Higher Vocational Education

Higher vocational education is key to developmental poverty alleviation. It provides opportunities for vulnerable groups to attain financial independence, exit welfare support, and contribute to economic growth.

Need for Employment Support

Employment support is essential. A vocational education program should be accompanied by a comprehensive placement scheme to ensure the disadvantaged individuals can secure meaningful employment. Continued support after placement is equally crucial to improving employment rate.

Benefits of Mentorship Programs

Mentor scheme has broad-ranging benefits. Mentor programs have the potential to solve individual difficulties in knowledge transfer, emotional support, and motivation for development. Pairing individuals with mentors can have similar positive effects.

Focus on Mental Health and Emotional Support

Mental health and emotional support are crucial. Financially disadvantaged groups are more likely to be mentally vulnerable as well. A comprehensive poverty alleviation project should address both material and mental well-being to provide holistic support for vulnerable individuals.

Suggestions on Experience Transfer

Close Collaboration of Local Organizations

Compared with material alleviation, developmental alleviation requires the collaboration with more stakeholders. The ideal project structure should resemble an industrial chain (e.g., Love Park–school–industry), where upstream organizations clarify the needs of the disadvantaged person, middle organizations and improve the person's abilities. In the meantime, downstream organizations match the person with appropriate development opportunities. Existing local organization framework should be engaged as much as possible, rather than creating new systems, to avoid a disjointed and unreasonable program design.

Social Support

Lack of personnel is a common problem for a poverty alleviation project. While China has partially solved this problem by utilizing CPC networks, while some countries may not have similar conditions. For organizations in these countries, the Tianjin case would be a good reference, where NGOs and general business firms are motivated to assist government initiative. Considering the popularity of social responsibility programs among many international companies, such an approach is also feasible overseas.

References

Chen, J. (2020). The youth changed by Qingmiao Class: From an Internet addicted teenager to a national level contestant, what have happened to an orphan in three years. *Xiangshengbao*.

Chen, L. (2019). *Research on governmental responsibility of the assistance for the older orphan* [Doctoral dissertation, Jilin University].

Huang, Y. (2021). From saplings to trees, vocational poverty alleviation has helped them grow in this way. *Hunan Gongren Bao*.

Hunan Architecture Senior Technical School. (2020a). *Present for the 40th anniversary: Vocational education poverty alleviation—Our orphan support case was selected as one of the global 110 poverty alleviation cases*.

Hunan Architecture Senior Technical School. (2020b). *Xinhua News Agency, CCTV, and many other central media entered our school to report vocational education poverty alleviation*.

Hunan Architecture Senior Technical School. (n.d.). *School summary: School basics*. http://www.hnjzgjjx.com/xygk/xyjj/

Hunan Provincial Bureau of Statistics & Survey Office of the National Bureau of Statistics in Hunan (Eds.). (2021). *2021 Hunan statistical yearbook*. Chinese Statistics Press. http://222.240.193.190/2021tjnj/indexeh.htm

Liu, Q., Gong, Y., & Li, M. (2018, August 21). *Jineng xin Luban, fupin xin fanben: Hunan Jianzhu Gaoji Jigong Xuexiao jineng fupin jishi 技能新鲁班，扶贫新范本!湖南建筑高级技工学校技能扶贫纪实* [Vocational new Luban, new model for poverty alleviation! Documentary of Hunan Architecture Senior Technical School skill-based poverty alleviation]. Sohu. https://www.sohu.com/a/249278668_99933053

Ministry of Civil Affairs. (2021). *2021 nian minzheng shiye fazhan tongji gongbao 2021 年民政事业发展统计公报* [Civil services development report 2021]. People's Republic of China. https://images3.mca.gov.cn/www2017/file/202208/2021mzsyfztjgb.pdf

Ministry of Human Resources and Social Security & Poverty Alleviation Office of the State Council. (2019, January 8). *Guanyu shenru tuijin jineng tuopin Qianxiao Xingdong de shishi yijian 关于深入推进技能脱贫千校行动的实施意见* [Implementation opinions on deeply promoting the Thousand Schools Action of skill-based poverty alleviation]. Zhongguo Zhengfu Wang. https://www.gov.cn/zhengce/zhengceku/2019-09/27/content_5433823.htm

Mo, C. (2021, December 20). *Cishan jiu gu, ci'ai manyuan: Xiangxi Zhou Ci'ai Yuan guan'ai gu'er jishi 慈善救孤 慈爱满园——湘西州慈爱园关爱孤儿纪实* [Rescue orphans with charity, fill the orphanage with love: A documentary of caring for orphans in the Love Park in Xiangxi Prefecture]. Hunan Daily. https://m.voc.com.cn/xhn/news/202112/17223755.html

Shang, X. (2008). *The system of social protection for vulnerable children in China 中国弱势儿童群体保护制度*. Social Sciences Literature Press.

Shang, X. & Li, X. (2015). Yong bu chengnian? Guojia yangyu de daling gu'er ruhe huode jingji duli 永不成年?国家养育的大龄孤儿如何获得经济独立 [Never growing up? How can national supported older orphans obtain financial independence]. *Shandong Social Sciences, 244*(12), 49–56. https://doi.org/10.14112/j.cnki.37-1053/c.2015.12.010

Skovdal, M., Mwasiaji, W., Webale, A., & Tomkins, A. (2011). Building orphan competent communities: experiences from a community-based capital cash transfer initiative in Kenya. *Health policy and planning, 26*(3), 233-241. https://doi.org/https://doi.org/10.1093/heapol/czq039

Yuan, G., Cheng, J., & Jia, L. (2018). Gu'er gaodeng zhiye jiaoyu guanli yu fuwu cunzai de wenti ji duice tanxi 孤儿高等职业教育管理与服务存在的问题及对策探析 [Orphan higher vocational education management and services discussion on the existing problems and corresponding strategies]. *Education and Vocation, 910*(6), 109–112. https://doi.org/10.13615/j.cnki.1004-3985.2018.06.022

Zhang, F., Yang, X., Hao, L., & Li, S. (2009). Gu'er xinli jiankang zhuangkuang diaocha fenxi yanjiu 孤儿心理健康状况调查分析研究 [Analysis on the mental health condition of orphans]. *Hebei Enterprise,* (12), 70–71. https://caod.oriprobe.com/articles/21519955/gu_er_xin_li_jian_kang_zhuang_kuang_diao_cha_fen_x.htm

Sichuan Poverty Alleviation Incentive Scheme

The Sichuan Poverty Alleviation Incentive Scheme, launched in 2014, was a pilot program implemented in 15 counties and districts of China's Sichuan Province. This program aimed to replace unconditional government subsidies with conditional cash rewards to incentivize excellent performance in production, increased labor income, and adherence to proper social etiquette.

The scheme not only involved villagers but also extended to engage business entities in certain areas of Sichuan Province. This extension created job opportunities for villagers, contributing to rural productivity, and also their income. The incentive scheme had also been introduced to government officials, tying it to the Key Performance Indicators (KPIs) of their works.

This program had benefited three key stakeholders in Sichuan Province: (a) villagers, (b) business entities, and (c) government officials. By providing incentives for performance and adherence to certain criteria, the scheme aimed to create a comprehensive system for rural economic development and improved villagers' living standards.

Background

As President Xi Jinping emphasized at the Central Conference on Poverty Alleviation and Development, "Poverty elimination and prosperity would ultimately be achieved through the impoverished people's hard work. We must give full play to the initiative of the grassroots officials and masses in poverty-stricken areas to encourage them to fight poverty with great passion." To deal with local villagers' reliance problem, the project tailored measures to enhance the impoverished households' enthusiasm and curb their sustainable reliance on government benefits. For example, instead of

International Poverty Reduction Center In China, *Poverty Alleviation Case Analysis In China*, SpringerBriefs on Case Studies of Sustainable Development,
https://doi.org/10.1007/978-981-97-4537-1_8

providing a minimum income guarantee, the scheme introduced a system of monthly awards that were linked to the household's income. This means that households with higher incomes would receive higher premium rewards, thereby incentivizing them to increase their earnings.

Focal Organization and Region

The Anti-poverty Policy Team Under the Survey and Research Centre for China Household Finance at the Southwestern University of Finance and Economics, a public welfare academic research institute established in 2010, conducts this program. This organization aims at tracking the dynamics of households' financial behaviour comprehensively and providing references for academic researchers and policymakers.

This program has already been implemented in 15 counties and districts in Southwest Sichuan Province, which is one of China's most severely impoverished regions. Due to poor transportation and unbalanced development, Sichuan has long been troubled by deep poverty.

The Key Challenges

The main challenge of this conditional cash transfer project lay in the deeply ingrained welfare-dependent mindset of impoverished households. Gan Li, the project leader, emphasized that "an increase in unconditional cash transfer tends to induce the problem of welfare dependency" (Gan 2019). This was precisely the issue which the project encountered in the implementation process.

In the past, the government provided comprehensive subsidies to rural households, including a minimum income guarantee, support for agricultural production, and healthcare guarantee, among others. However, these subsidies, coupled with a lack of incentives, gave rise to the development of a welfare dependency mindset among those impoverished households. An illustrative example of this can be seen in how households approached the minimum income guarantee. Fearing the potential loss of cash transfers that accompanied an increase in income, some households actively resisted efforts to alleviate poverty. Consequently, even if some had managed to escape poverty, they deliberately chose to regress and become dependent on welfare support once again. This observation is further supported by data on China's per capita disposable income from 2013 to 2016, which indicates a 7% rise in rural households' disposable income, and a decrease in income among the poorest households.

The Solutions

The challenges of the poverty in Sichuan were addressed through a multi-layered approach, which included the following strategies:

Poverty Alleviation Among the Villagers

An award scheme was introduced based on the income of impoverished families. The amount of the incentive varied according to different levels of household income. For households classified as severely impoverished with CNY 400 per capital per month, the incentive scheme was designed in the way which the subsidizing amount would be calculated proportionally to their income. However, till the monthly labor income reached CNY 1,000, the amount of the incentive gradually decreased.

Income was not the sole criterion for evaluating incentive award. The practice of good manners and proper social etiquette, as well as avoidance of overspending on ceremonies, gambling, drug usage, or overdependency on social security support, were also considered. These additional criteria aimed at fostering a positive culture within the community and promoting communal values.

The scheme was implemented through a well-managed and efficient administrative process. From eligible participants' application to authority review and approval, the procedure was streamlined to ensure that the whole process could be completed in a timely manner. There was mechanism to oversee the entire implementation process and to ensure relevant accountability.

In certain cases, the incentive programs succeeded in motivating villagers to explore higher-value agricultural varieties (e.g., tea, vegetables, and fruits), to convert farmland and forestland, and to engage in animal breeding businesses. These efforts contributed to a significant increase in households' income, improving their financial situation and enabling them to afford a higher standard of living.

Secondary Industry Development and Job Creation by Business Entities

New mechanisms were introduced to promote broad societal engagement.

First, an incentive policy was established to encourage business entities to set up poverty alleviation workshops. In addition to the employment subsidy, a onetime incentive for establishing poverty alleviation workshops and loan benefits, the workshops were supported by services which include free pre-job training for the workers, entrepreneurship training and guidance.

Second, the financial subsidies for business and industrial development for the commercial entities were tied to the number of poor laborers employed.

Third, to address difficulties in borrowing money for rural industrial development, the enterprise or the cooperative with poor employees was provided with a local government-guaranteed loans.

Within the above mechanism, three types of industrial development models were set up to widen the channel of job creation: factory-format poverty alleviation workshop. crowd-funding cooperative to which poor households could contribute land, capital, labor, or technologies, and flexible employment poverty workshop, with a focus on labor-intensive enterprises utilizing idle land, houses, and warehouses in areas with a higher population of poverty or resettlement. Production and business activities such as manufacturing clothing and textiles, electronics, handicrafts, and agricultural product processing developed quickly to address the employment challenges faced by the poor rural population.

To achieve stable employment, the following service provisions were put in place:

1. An online-offline job matching service which was enabled by means of "Internet+" and WeChat groups, was developed. Supported by comprehensive database, this service facilitated the matching of employment demand between villagers and enterprises;
2. Job-specific training programs were provided, utilizing integrated resources. This included ecological and sustainable business and tourism training through farmers' evening schools and field classrooms. This provided villagers with short-term practical technical training which suits their job request;
3. Overall regional employment conditions are closely monitored. This includes individual employment status, remuneration payments as agreed, and training demand, etc. Any unfavorable change in these conditions were promptly identified, while ensuring the protection of the remuneration's rights and interests of the poor. Low-skilled jobs would become available to those who were unemployed.

Incentive for Goal-Oriented Governance

A targeted incentive scheme was implemented for the government officials, with specific KPIs assigned to officials of different ranks. Successful officials who achieved their targets were given priority for future promotions and enjoyed guaranteed benefits, commendations from the organization, and awards such as commemorative items.

Relationship to SDG and ESG

The successful implementation of this project significantly increased impoverished households' annual income, which reaches the United Nations' SDGs. With the mindset change of impoverished households from welfare-dependent to self-dependent, monthly household income in the Wutongqiao district increased by CNY 559 ($84) per month and household expenditure increased by CNY 436 (approximately USD 60) per month. This implies higher consumption and an improved living standard for the impoverished households through the implementation of this cash award incentive program. This result not only shows the projects' potential to "end poverty" and promote "higher living standards" sustainably but also displays China's determination and attempt to "reduce inequalities within countries." This is consistent with the United Nations' SDGs (United Nations n.d.).

This project focuses on poverty alleviation and tries to promote education. As stated by the project leader, Gan Li, "One important reason accounted for the poverty is that education is commonly undervalued by impoverished households". With the aim of blocking intergenerational transmission of poverty, the Youth Education Promotion Program (青少年教育促进计划) has a part in this conditional cash transfer project. By offering cash rewards to those who made significant progress in school, students are deeply motivated. The principal of the primary school where the program was implemented said, "This project is quite effective in building up the student's confidence as well as motivating their inner study impetus". Currently, this project has covered nearly 93,000 students and inspired them to devote themselves to studying. The remarkable result achieved by this project in this overall low-level education district echoed precisely the UNSDG goal of "quality education".

Case Analysis

In this case, a comprehensive plan was implemented, engaging key stakeholders. The approach consisted of not just a single initiative, but a step-by-step plan with long-term strategies.

For the rural impoverished households, the plan began with incentive schemes, resulting in immediate improvements in villagers' employment and the corresponding rewards for them. As their enthusiasm grew, support was provided expand their capabilities and business opportunities. Higher income was made possible through various channels, including land lease, investments, and fair labor remuneration.

For alternative employment of the villagers, business entities were incentivised and subsidized financially, plus loan guarantees provided, to establish industrial workshops and generate job opportunities. These workshops, established in commercial or cooperative formats, have not only alleviated poverty but also fostered local economic development.

All these efforts were facilitated by various services to ensure efficient supervision, management, and operations. They are under the government, which itself had its own incentive concept and scheme.

International Case

Conditional transfer programs have been implemented in at least 16 countries in the world. The Earned Income Tax Credit (EITC) program in the United States is believed to be the most representative one which inspired the Chinese incentive-compatible program.

Established in 1975, the EITC offered tax rebates to low-income households. It is the most extensive targeted income transfer program in the United States (Smeeding et al. 2000, p. 2).

The EITC is offered to eligible claimants in the form of income tax liability reduction, a year-end cash payment, or a combination of the two (Falk 2014, p. 3). The credit amount is determined by the number of claimants' qualifying children and earned income (Falk 2014, p. 3). "In general, the EITC amount increases with earnings up to a point (the maximum earned income eligible for the credit), and then remains unchanged for a certain bracket of income (the plateau), and then (beginning at the phase-out income level) gradually decreases to zero as earnings continue to increase" (Falk 2014, p. 3). In 2011, every recipient of EITC received a USD2,254 in subsidy on average (Falk 2014, p. 9).

These two programs are similar. For example, in the Wutongqiao Experiment-Labor Income Reward Plan, the determinant of the cash reward is also the household's last month's earnings. Proportional to the monthly earnings at a fixed rate, the reward increased with earnings before reaching the maximum level and remained the same for the plateau stage before it diminished and went down to zero. It meant that the household was no longer eligible for this income reward plan.

However, to make the plan more appealing and feasible, adjustments and amendments are made to align with local conditions. Two major differences between cash reward incentive programs and the EITC program are the calculation method and distribution frequency. "First, the calculation is different: After all the household members have reported their earnings, the earnings will be accumulated on the household level. Next, per capita earnings will be calculated by dividing the total earnings by family size. Then, the reward per person will be calculated by applying the rules in the three-stage scheme. The final amount of reward will be the reward per person multiplied by the number in the household". Second, the Chinese cash reward program is distributed monthly instead of annual distribution.

Best Practice Case Reference: New Folk Style Development Leadership Group Office at Ankang Village in Shanxi Province (陕西安康新民风建设领导小组办公室) on Grassroots Governance (基层治理)

In Ankang village, Shanxi Province, not all impoverished individuals were actively striving to overcome poverty. Some had accustomed to their impoverished state and lacked the motivation or initiative to change their poor situation.

To foster a culture that values honest reflection on villagers' own situation so as to respond accordingly, emphasizes family responsibility, promotes better individual financial management, encourages hard work, and cultivates harmonious social interactions— they had drawn upon the adoption and promotion of traditional virtues.

Since 2017, various events and the media initiatives have been implemented to promote traditional virtues in the region. As a result, the poor population decreased from 581,000 in 2015 to 33,000 in 2019, with poverty incidence down from 23.5% to 1.3%.

Several incentives were implemented to exert a positive influence:

1. Representative cases were selected. Hardworking villagers and disabled individuals with positive mindsets and capabilities were selected as role models and celebrated through commendation activities;
2. A morale points system was introduced at "kindness supermarkets" and "ethical banks," where individuals could accumulate points and exchange them for gifts. It conveyed the message that efforts would be duly rewarded; and
3. Repeat offenders of negative behavior faced reasonable penalties to discourage them on these negative mentality and activity.

The message and concept were promoted through both online and offline channels, including theoretical education, conventional and online news coverage, social outreach, as well as art and cultural activities. By instilling traditional virtues and improving people's mindsets, a solid foundation was laid for successful poverty alleviation and the implementation of new initiatives for rural revitalization.

References

Falk, G., Crandall-Hollick, M. L. (2014). The earned income tax credit (EITC): an overview. Congressional Research Service

Gan, L. (2019). '甘犁:解决相对贫困需建立激励相容的现金转移支付制度 ' https://www.sohu.com/a/354713380_637114

Smeeding, T, M., Phillips, K. R., O'Connor, M. (2000). The EITC: Expectation, knowledge, use, and economic and social mobility. Center for Policy Research Working Paper No. 13

Dingbian Menu-Based Big Data Management System

Chinese President Xi Jinping often mentions targeted poverty reduction and poverty alleviation together. He indicates four key elements to achieve targeted poverty reduction, with the fourth element described as how to target poverty alleviation. First, there needs a timetable for an orderly poverty exit. Second, it is to set a buffer period between apparent poverty alleviation and the discontinuation of related policies. The third is to implement strict evaluations, in accordance with the poverty alleviation standard. Fourth, it is to implement the practice of household registration, so as to get rid of poverty.

—Xi Jinping, speech, national commendation conference on poverty eradication, Xinhua

Dingbian, a county of Yulin City, Shanxi Province, spans an area of 6,920 square kilometers and holds the distinction of being the birthplace of the Luo River. The county has abundant natural resources. For instance, its oil reserves reaches 1.618 billion tons, making Dingbian the top counties in China in terms of regional oil and gas production capacity. Despite the favorable natural resources, Dingbian county was identified as a national-designated poverty county in the period 1986–2018.

One of the leading causes of poverty was the county's local climate. Dingbian county has a typical temperate semi-arid continental monsoon climate, characterized by low rainfall and sandy conditions. Consequently, crop yields are adversely affected, while certain villagers faced water shortages. Limited production of agricultural goods due to inefficiency was another challenge the county faced. Moreover, Dingbian was home to over 10,000 impoverished individuals, necessitating the rational and efficient allocation of resources as a critical consideration for poverty alleviation. These obstacles, while not unique to Dingbian, are common in many other regions.

However, Dingbian faced a distinct set of obstacles which required specific attention in order to lift the county out of poverty:

1. The county primarily acted as a conduit, merely receiving and passing on documents from superior authorities to lower-level officials, without adequately considering the unique needs of individual poor households.

International Poverty Reduction Center In China, *Poverty Alleviation Case Analysis In China*, SpringerBriefs on Case Studies of Sustainable Development,
https://doi.org/10.1007/978-981-97-4537-1_9

2. Poverty-stricken households were overwhelmed with excessive information.
3. Impoverished households adopted a passive approach and lacked the agency to actively choose the most suitable plan for their circumstances, even when government officials tried to implement poverty alleviation policies.

The Focal Issue

Poverty alleviation projects, initiated or sponsored by the government, are often arranged by superior authorities to inferior ones, who has to adhere closely to these guidelines during implementation. However, these comprehensive yet general plans merely serve as guidelines, which are insufficient to address the specific needs of individual households and lift them out of poverty. Different governmental departments may issue a multitude of documents, with information sometimes not coordinated, creating an information overload that was challenging for inferior authorities and poverty-stricken individuals to navigate.

To address this challenge, Chinese President XI Jinping introduced the strategy of targeted poverty alleviation in March 2014 in his speech at Guizhou, aiming to eliminate the root causes of poverty. In the same year, the Chinese government officially adopted this strategy. Through the announcement by the State Council, it was emphasized that officials had to "implement targeted measures to ensure assistance reaches poverty-stricken villages and households." The strategy has three main stages.

Firstly, precise identification of impoverished individuals is crucial and is achieved through a national registration system. Secondly, targeted assistance is provided, taking into account the specific needs and circumstances of each individual. This is often accomplished by pairing the individual with a local government official, who then becomes responsible for eradicating poverty for the designated person. However, this process requires cooperation from those households or individuals involved. Lastly, accurate assessment of the poverty alleviation efforts is crucial, and this is conducted by third-party agencies.

The Focal Organization

As the driving force for change, the People's Government of Dingbian has set up a number of internal units, including the Administrative Secretary Unit, Conference Communications Unit, Logistics Support Unit, Office Integrated Unit, and Confidential Files Unit. Additionally, it comprises various division units, including the Local Financial Service Center, Office Service Center, Center for Caring for the Next Generation of Work, E-government Information Center, City Creation Job Service Center, and Weather Modification Service Center. The primary focus of the local government is the administration of state affairs, internal affairs, and social public affairs. Acting as a social lubricant, its main responsibility is to ensure the coordinated and orderly development of various economic and social processes.

In 2014, the People's Government of Dingbian reported fiscal revenues amounting to CNY 3,548.86 million, with expenses reaching CNY 3,089.57 million. The government displayed a commitment to enriching people's welfare. It invested CNY 11.86 billion in key areas including agricultural industrialization, urban infrastructure, and other fields.

The Solutions

National Strategy: Targeted Poverty Alleviation (TPA)

XI Jinping, the General Secretary of the CPC, first introduced the concept of targeted poverty alleviation, as part of his vision to address poverty in China. The first goal of XI Jinping's vision of the Four Comprehensives is to comprehensively build a "fairly well-off society." XI Jinping frequently emphasizes the need to address rural poverty, as China's development into a society of fairly well-off hinges on this issue. In 2014, the Chinese government officially adopted the targeted poverty alleviation strategy. In the State Council report in 2014, it was highlighted about the importance of local governments consolidating poverty alleviation resources and implementing targeted measures to ensure that assistance reaches poverty-stricken areas and households.

Menu-Based Policy in Dingbian County

The People's Government of Dingbian county adopted the targeted poverty alleviation strategy outlined previously and customized it to create "menu-based" poverty alleviation measures. First, the county developed a menu of measures which can be easily understood and implemented in conjunction with specific working conditions. Second, based on the circumstances of each household, support officials actively assist poor households to make choices from the menu a shortlist of specific programs and benefits relevant to different low-income households. Throughout, an integrated big data platform is used to manage the complete execution process. Finally, there is account-based trace management to ensure the openness and transparency of assistance and support measures.

The following is a summary of how poverty alleviation initiatives were carried out using the menu-based policy in Dingbian county (Fig. 1).

Considering the unique working circumstances, the county devised a menu of actions which were easy to grasp and simple to implement. Following research and analysis by considering the characteristics in their actual work, pertinent government departments developed policies which were tailored to the specific characteristics of

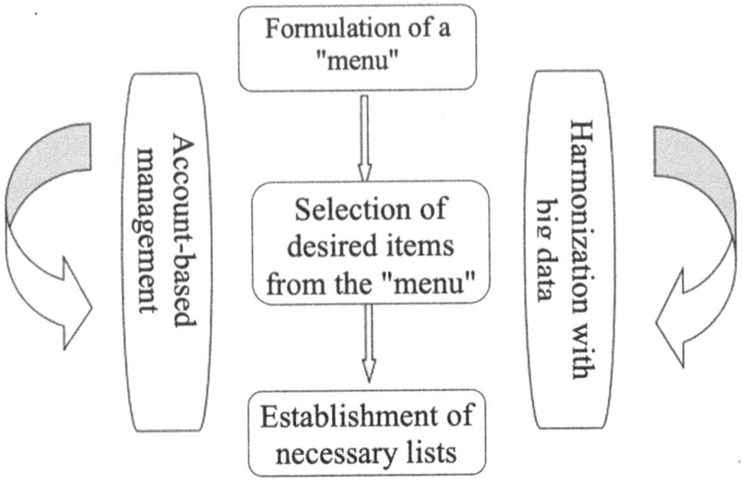

Fig. 1 "Menu-Based" execution of poverty alleviation measures

their work. To ensure widespread dissemination, the Poverty Alleviation Steering Group of the county then compiled these policies into a comprehensive schedule, often referred to as the "menu." In 2017, more than 20,000 copies of the menu were distributed throughout the county to ensure that each poor household received a copy.

Based on their financial and housing circumstances, the support officials actively assisted poor households in selecting suitable options from the menu. The officials suggested potential menu items, while the impoverished individuals had the autonomy to choose the options they found appealing.

Lists were created to outline the entitlements and benefits for low-income households. Each household in need received a customized list of such benefits and policies, which support officials attached to their houses. These lists assisted low-income households in comprehending the policies and determining the resources available to them. They also provided clear overview of policy implementation progress and the outcomes of aid and support. Various measures were taken to ensure that village and household records and data were accurate (Fig. 2).

A big data platform was used to administer the whole execution process in a coordinated way. To ensure interoperability with the municipal and provincial governments' systems for addressing poverty, as well as the data on poverty alleviation held by or related to governmental agencies, towns, villages, and county households, an innovative big data platform was established. A mobile phone application allowed those who provided assistance and support to upload data of poverty and the impact of their efforts. Authorities could get access to these data anytime, anyplace, with desktops or mobile devices. They could also look for routes to poor families directly. Besides improving the accuracy and timeliness of information updates, this big data platform significantly lightened the load on support officials (Fig. 3).

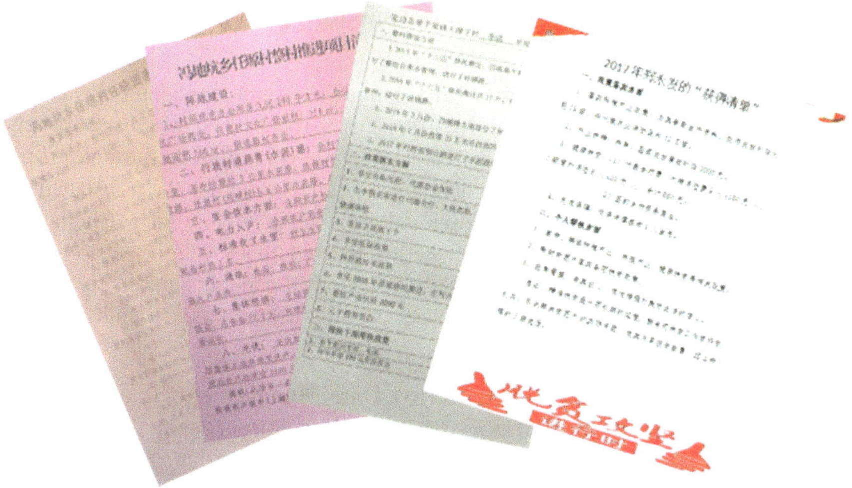

Fig. 2 Lists received by Dingbian county's impoverished villages and households

Fig. 3 Big data platform for poverty alleviation in Dingbian county

The transparency and openness of aid and support measures were enhanced through the implementation of account-based trace management, as follows:

Establishment of Dynamic Databases. Accounts were created, maintained, and upgraded, transitioning from simple sheets to category-based systems. Dynamic databases were developed at the county, township, and village levels, categorizing poverty alleviation workers, projects, and the underprivileged population. These databases accurately recorded assistance and support measures, letters and calls, social stability, and other relevant information. Additionally, a comprehensive record management system was implemented, ensuring interconnectedness and facilitating practical decision-making, robust implementation by support officials, and ultimately achieveing successful outcomes.

Standardized and Active Account Management. Account management was standardized and transformed from a passive to an active process. The progress of poverty alleviation measures was dynamically tracked by support officials through prompt revision and supplementation of the accounts to reflect whether the assistance and support for targeted impoverished individuals was accurately defined, whether the poverty measures were in place, and whether the outcomes were observable in a comprehensive manner. With these initiatives, both the public and every official involved in the assistance and support process could access the accounts and learn about their status.

Qualitative Changes through Quantitative Data Management. To achieve qualitative changes through quantitative data management, accounts were removed from benchmarking upon completion of relevant tasks. Regular evaluations were conducted to monitor the progress of incomplete projects and eliminate completed tasks from the accounts. For incomplete projects, causes were examined and identified, and implementation strategies were modified accordingly to ensure timely completion. In 2017, the county issued more than 100 documents including Notices on Supervision and Correction for Targeted Poverty Alleviation, Letters on Supervised Execution, Bulletins of Supervision and Inspection, and Letters of Reminder. It made more than 30 corrective cases according to self-reviews and feedback from the provincial and municipal governments, while removing 369 completed items from the accounts. Every effort was made to ensure timely completion of tasks, resolution of issues, and adherence to allocated time frames. Improved supervision and assessment to encourage task completion, measure the actual impact of labor, and ensure compliance with relevant rules. The accounts underwent scrutiny, examination, testing, and verification, demonstrating the tangible impact of poverty reduction efforts (Fig. 4).

Case Analysis

Positive Effects

The "menu-based" poverty alleviation strategy has brought positive impacts in two main aspects, higher working efficiency, and better living standards for the impoverished households.

The first positive impact was the increase in working efficiency. With menu-based poverty alleviation, the public and the authorities had access to a detailed schedule of pertinent policies. The number of documents has decreased, and it was simple to understand. The menu-based strategy was supported by a ground-breaking big data platform for alleviating poverty. This has greatly decreased the workload of the

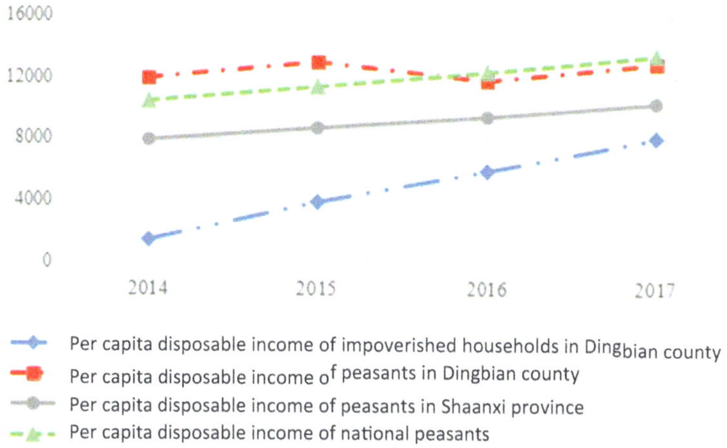

Fig. 4 Comparison of per capita incomes between rural residents in Dingbian county, Shaanxi province, and the whole country between 2014 and 2017 (Unit: CNY)

officials who are in charge of providing aid and support and significantly enhanced the timeliness and quality of information updates. Furthermore, menu-based poverty alleviation created fundamental records which could withstand inspection, questioning, scrutiny, and checking, ensuring practical decision-making, solid execution, and truthful results.

In terms of living standards, Dingbian county made significant progress in poverty reduction. By 2017, Dingbian county had implemented a 15-year free education program and offered teaching lessons to families with disabled children in their homes. The county's whole impoverished population, who were protected by major disease insurance, took part in the New Cooperative Medical System for rural inhabitants. The government was responsible for paying the New Cooperative Medical System for all the impoverished people. Every resident had access to clean water and secure housing. Furthermore, all administrative villages had 4G telecommunications coverage, while 100% of households had a guaranteed power supply, and paved roads. In Dingbian county, the proportion of the impoverished population fell to 1.13% in 2017. From 2014 to 2017, the average per capita income of the registered poor households climbed by nearly 30%, which was higher than the national average rate.

Statistical measurements were used to evaluate the impacts of the poverty alleviation program. Figure 5 shows the per capita household income of Dingbian county over time. The average income for town and village households was CNY 30,911 and CNY 11,829, respectively, in 2014. Both increased by around CNY 2,000 in 2015, after the implementation of this targeted alleviation program. The figures showed some decreasing trends between 2014 and 2018, the trends rose, in general. From 2014 to 2021, the per capita rural household income increased by more than 1.5 times while the income increase of town households was about 1.14 times. From the educational perspective, the number of enrolled students in primary schools was used for comparison. Figure 6 shows a faster increasing rate between every two years since 2013. The number kept rising from 19,324 in 2014 to 28,951 in 2019. In the medical and health aspect, the number of beds in hospitals and health centers was used as a reference for evaluation. As shown in Fig. 7, it is apparent that the bed offerings increased sharply after 2008. Although the number of beds reduced slightly from the peak point in 2017 (1,730,000) to 1,598,000 in 2018, it grew to 1,635,000 in 2019. All these general patterns appeared to indicate that the targeted efforts to reduce poverty had successfully improved the incomes of the impoverished people in Dingbian county.

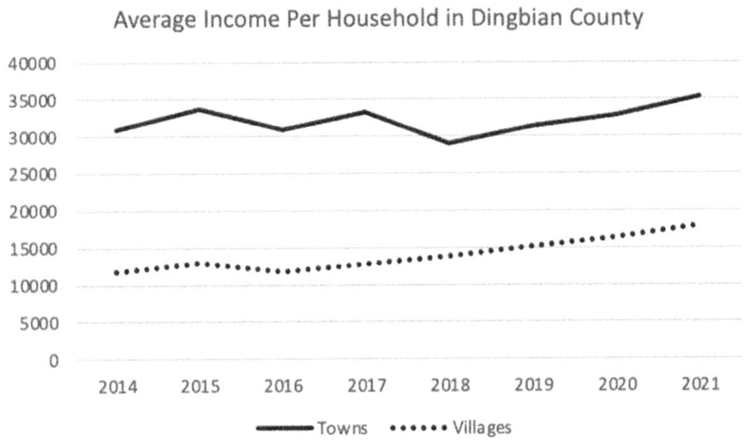

Fig. 5 Average income per household in Dingbian county (Unit: CNY)

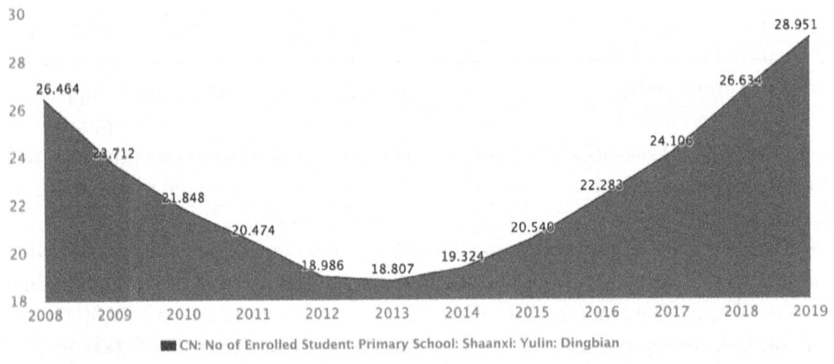

Fig. 6 Number of enrolled students in primary school in Dingbian county. *Note* Source from CEIC data https://www.ceicdata.com/en/china/number-of-enrolled-student-primary-school-county-level-region/no-of-enrolled-student-primary-school-shaanxi-yulin-dingbian

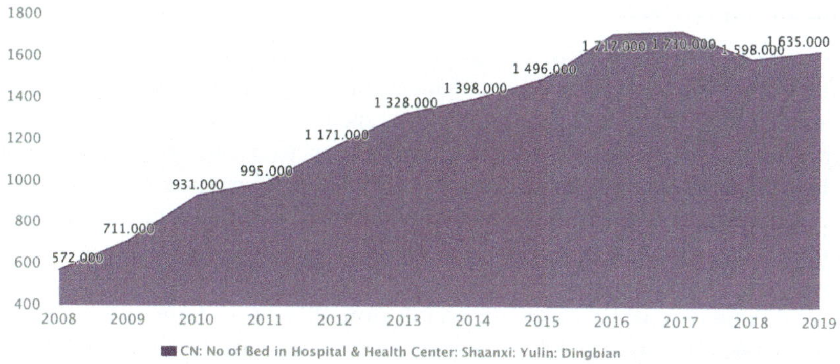

Fig. 7 Number of beds in hospitals and health center in Dingbian county. *Note* Source from CEIC data https://www.ceicdata.com/en/china/number-of-bed-in-hospital--health-center-county-level-region/no-of-bed-in-hospital--health-center-shaanxi-yulin-dingbian

The assessment of the percentage of the population in poverty and income inequality in Yulin Township provides the perspective for comparison. The findings indicate a significant reduction in poverty and relatively minor changes in income inequality.

In terms of poverty reduction, as shown in Fig. 8, the percentage of population in poverty (poverty rate) in Yulin Township remainged relatively stable between 2014 and 2015, with a slight decrease from 14.27% to 14.06%. By the end of 2016, it decreased to 13.83%. However, since the rollout of the series of targeted poverty reduction programs in 2016, the poverty rate started to decrease significantly. In 2017, the poverty rate had dropped to 9.15%., and it further reduced to 0.85% by the end of 2018. Only 76 households and 163 people were still living in poverty in 2018. The date suggests that poverty in Yulin Township was on track to be officially eliminated by the end of 2019. This indicated the success of the focused industrial poverty alleviation initiative in reducing poverty levels.

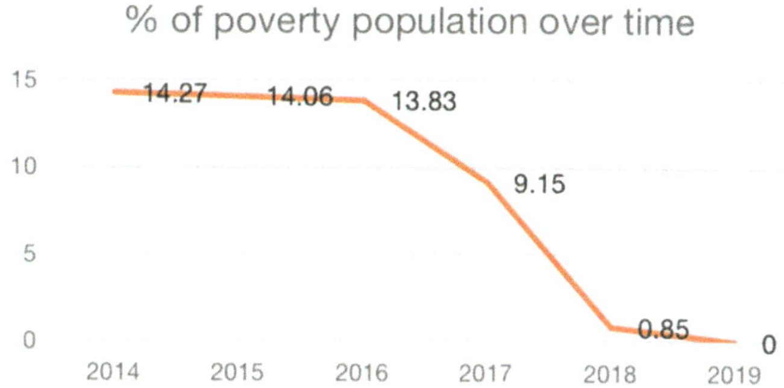

Fig. 8 Percentage of poverty population in Yulin

Contingent Effects

After the menu-based policy was implemented in Dingbian, the county government invested CNY 80.225 million to build plastic sheds, sheep sheds, family farms, and agricultural machinery, and paid agricultural insurance on behalf of poor households to help them develop a breeding industry. This indirectly promoted the transformation and upgrade of the county's breeding industry. In addition, there had been an improvement in farming practices and yields. As one of the six largest potato-growing counties in China, Dingbian's annual potato production is 1 million tons, and 80% of local farmers consider it as a major cash crop. Previously, farmers were not able to profit much from planting potatoes owing to disease, marketing, and other factors. Since the development of the menu-based poverty alleviation strategy, the county experienced full integration of its primary, secondary, and tertiary industries and the production of sales of potatoes had improved subsequently. In August 2017, the People's Government of Dingbian combined target poverty alleviation efforts with tourism by launching the "10,000 mu of flowers" and "Dingbian safflower buckwheat festival." It allowed poor villages to vigorously develop leisure agriculture, sightseeing tourism, and other new forms of business. Eventually, the average household income of poor households in the region increased by CNY 5,000. Studies have shown that developments in the agricultural industry can provide a stable and sustainable income for farmers and achieve long-term and sustainable poverty reduction results.

Potential Issues

In theory, the most efficient way of eliminating poverty with a given budget is to focus efforts on disadvantaged groups. However, the implementation of tailored policies is more difficult in practice and can have unexpected outcomes due to several complicating factors. First, it is difficult to precisely identify impoverished individuals or households due to imperfect information. Traditionally, it has been done through self-targeting and surveys collected from households regarding their living conditions. However, these methods are often expensive. On average, identification expenditure accounts for 22% of the total program cost as opposed to 30% for monitoring and evaluation-related activities. Moreover, the long-term sustainability and effectiveness of Dingbian's menu-based poverty alleviation strategy need to be examined. This was a common concern about most targeted poverty alleviation policies. Support officials and local government agencies need to ensure that these policies can remain in effect for a certain time after the individual or household exist the poverty. At the same time, sufficient supervision should be undertaken to consolidate results.

Best Practice Case Reference: The Poverty Alleviation and Development Leading Group Office of Linyi City in Shandong Province (山东省临沂市扶贫开发领导小组办公室)—Poverty Alleviation Asset Management framework

From 2016 to 2019, more than 2 billion yuan of poverty alleviation funds were utilized to assist over 450,000 individuals. Given the vast amount of funds involved, the challenge lay in managing them effectively to ensure the sustained impact and benefits for impoverished populations.

The Poverty Alleviation and Development Leading Group Office of Linyi City in Shandong Province established a poverty alleviation fund asset management mechanism based on the "four rights separation" principle: the village owns poverty alleviation assets collectively, operational rights are granted to impoverished households, income rights are secured for contracted impoverished households, and the town government implements supervisory rights.

A clear definition of poverty asset ownership was a prerequisite for strengthening asset management. Operational assets were specified by different industrial development funds as needed. Except for assets with specific designated purposes, all poverty alleviation assets were collectively owned by the village and recorded with a certificate. In Wangou Town, for example, this included greenhouses, photovoltaic power stations, and planting fields.

The operational rights of the assets were contracted to impoverished households who were responsible for implementation and had to consider market conditions, including competition. Together with the collaboration with industry-leading enterprises, professional cooperatives, and e-commerce, it improved the quality and effectiveness of industrial projects.

The income generated from poverty alleviation assets through leasing primarily assisted contracting impoverished households, with the remaining portion allocated for the development of public welfare projects within the village, particularly those benefiting the elderly, weak, disabled, or ill individuals who lack the ability to work. Impoverished individuals with labor capabilities were offered public service positions such as security, forest fire prevention, and solar panel maintenance. A differentiated distribution mechanism with classification ensured precise distribution based on household circumstances.

The local authority was delegated the role of supervision, which included managing poverty alleviation funds and assets, integrating platforms with real-time information access for dynamic adjustment, and auditing village accounts to ensure that poverty alleviation funds and assets were effectively managed. This guaranteed transparency, fairness, and justice throughout the operation of poverty alleviation assets.

International Comparative Studies

Conditional cash transfer programs have been widely adopted by more than 70 countries around the world as a form of targeted poverty alleviation. As defined by the World Bank, conditional cash transfer programs aim to reduce poverty by making welfare programs conditional upon the recipients' actions. Therefore, the donor, typically governments or non-profit organizations, only transferred money to persons who meet certain criteria.

Brazil's Bolsa Família social welfare program is a notable example of conditional cash transfer programs. The main objectives of this program included reducing inequality and poverty rates by providing a minimum level for impoverished households. Moreover, it aimed to improve human capital through education and health care. Brazil's Bolsa Família wished to empower beneficiaries by connecting them with complementary services like social assistance and employment training programs. To be eligible, child beneficiaries need to ensure that they meet certain levels of school attendance and have the required vaccines. Local governments and officials collect information to verify compliance, and the federal government then disbursed the cash transfer of R$70.00 (approximately USD 35) per individual per month.

Similar to Dingbian's menu-based poverty alleviation approach, the Bolsa Família program requires tracking progress and ensuring that beneficiaries met the conditions for continued support. In December 2006, Brazil implemented a system to manage and keep track of the program was launched. The system utilized advanced technology like satellites and radio waves to connect the internet, and enabled communication with municipalities, even in distant areas with limited phone or electricity access. Dingbian, on the other hand, took it one step further to incorporate the latest advanced technology such as big data.

Overall, the Bolsa Família program has been highly successful in Brazil. By 2015, it supported over 13 million families, with an average payment of R$167.15 (approximately USD 35) per month. Despite its relatively low cost (equivalent to 0.5% of Brazil's GDP), the program achieved significant result. It reduced poverty rates by approximately 15% and extreme poverty by 25%. Concurrently, it contributed to a more than 50% decrease in infant mortality which was caused by undernourishment and diarrhoea. Furthermore, the passing rate of students in secondary education also surged from 75.7% to 79.7%.

Key Learnings

Relationship to UN DGs and Environmental, Social, and Governance (ESG) Factors

Poverty is a pervasive global issue that impacts a significant portion of the population, and addressing poverty is a primary goal of development programs worldwide. The inclusion of the SDGs agenda in National Long-Term Development Plan highlights the commitment to poverty eradication (RPJPN 2005–2025).

Accurate poverty data is crucial since poverty is the primary consideration in the planning process of these initiatives, as well as the accuracy of determining the eligibility of individuals to participate in these programs. The effectiveness of targeting, which refers to the efficiency and accuracy in directing resources, assistance, and interventions to specific groups or individuals in poverty alleviation, plays a vital role in determining the success of achieving the SDG target of poverty eradication.

With the targeted poverty alleviation program carried out in Dingbian county, the people who would receive benefits were accurately identified. By mobilizing resources from different sources, a menu-based program was implemented to tackle the poverty issue. The poor and the vulnerable were given the right to choose from opportunities of economic resources, access to essential services, the use of modern technologies, and financial services. By the end of 2017, Dingbian county had tailored assistance programs for 9,765 poor households and set up 9,765 access lists of policies for poor households and 226 access lists at the village level. These had successfully provided more than 30,000 family projects for suitable development.

In relation to the SDGs, Dingbian county's menu-based policy successfully helped to achieve the first goal of SDG in "No poverty." By eradicating extreme poverty, Dingbian county had contributed to global poverty reduction. Taking relevant figures in 2017 as an example; a total of 32,718 people from 8,480 households in 78 impoverished villages were lifted out of poverty. The per capita disposable income per capita of the poor households reached CNY 8,008, and the poverty incidence dropped to 1.13%. Also, with the great investments in basic needs, including health care, education, water and sanitation, and so forth, other SDGs were attained at the same time. Such goals included zero hunger, good health and well-being, quality education, and clean water and sanitation.

Considering environmental, social, and governance (ESG) factors, social and economic pillars were important for reducing poverty, and long-term strategic thinking was essential. In other words, achieving the No poverty goal also depends on the environmental component. For instance, investments and initiatives which failed to conserve the natural world and run the risk of biodiversity loss can further impoverish the poor by disrupting agricultural income. Therefore, for individual firms and organizations, they can also think about how community outreach programs and positive involvement can actively contribute to poverty reduction in all its aspects. For example, they can invest in SDGs like health care, affordable and clean energy, innovation and infrastructure, clean water and sanitation, and climate action, which are sensitive and effective. As a result, it may help lift some people out of absolute poverty and lessen the climate change impact on the most vulnerable groups.

Concluding Thoughts

Overall, China's targeted approach to poverty alleviation had yielded considerable success. In the case of Dingbian county, the menu-based and IT-enabled poverty alleviation measures helped to lift more than 30,000 people out of poverty. From an economic perspective, it contributed to the rise in average per capita income of the registered poor households by nearly 30%. Besides, there were numerous indirect impacts. The county's breeding, agriculture, and tourism sectors have all witnessed notable improvements.

Nevertheless, it is important to acknowledge potential challenges, including filtering costs, that may arise with this approach. Long-term sustainability and effectiveness should also be monitored to ensure continued success. Exploring international alternatives, Brazil stood out for its targeted poverty alleviation policies, exemplified by the Bolsa Família social welfare program. This initiative employed conditional cash transfers to precisely combat poverty while generating additional benefits such as improved healthcare and education, particularly for impoverished individuals, especially children.

Guzhen Agricultural Product E-Commerce Development

E-commerce, the online trading of goods, has become widespread in both urban and rural areas of China since the 2000s. The simplicity of conducting transactions and the of well-developed logistics network have enabled individuals and companies to vastly expand their business categories and profit margins. Despite the life-changing impact of the e-commerce industry in Chinese cities, the industry's expansion has been limited in rural China due to a lack of logistics support and inadequate access to updated information. As a result, e-commerce was not commonly considered a means of poverty alleviation in rural China until recently.

In 2018, the start of the Agricultural Food Station (农粮驿站) project initiated the development of e-commerce in rural China. It in turn paved a new way to alleviate poverty. Although there were difficulties in certain areas, the villagers and poverty alleviation committee have found ways to overcome the problems and efficiently used e-commerce to deal with poverty.

The Focal Issue in China

The e-commerce industry in China began in the early 2000s. The early participants, JD and Alibaba, mainly targeted China's first and second-tier cities, taking advantage of the "rising manufacturing and trading" amid a rapid economic growth context. With the increasing purchasing power of individuals, e-commerce firms had to develop strategies to build consumer trust in the e-commerce business model.

Although the middle-class consumers and firms benefited from a wider diversity of goods, consumers and producers from lower-income regions were not enjoying the benefits of e-commerce due to the lack of logistics infrastructure. Products like vegetables and meats could not be transported efficiently throughout the country. This limited farmers' ability to join the e-commerce market.

International Poverty Reduction Center In China, *Poverty Alleviation Case Analysis In China*, SpringerBriefs on Case Studies of Sustainable Development,
https://doi.org/10.1007/978-981-97-4537-1_10

In 2015, with the introduction of Pinduoduo (拼多多), a company which specifically targeted China's lower-income and rural markets, (Meemi 2022) brought attention to the immense potential of these rural regions as a market for e-commerce. This in turn provided more opportunities to local farmers with new avenues of sales, which offered higher efficiency comparing with traditional channel such as the physical market.

The Focal Village

Guzhen County (固镇县), located in China's Anhui Province, is characterized by its abundance of river streams, fertile soil, and moderate temperatures. These natural features have facilitated the growth of various crops such as lotus root, water chestnut, and reeds, as well as the rearing of livestock including cows, fish, and goats. (IPRCC 2021) The county's primary industry has been growing at an average rate of 5% (IPRCC 2021). Unlike many other counties, Guzhen has maintained stable population growth alongside its expanding industrial sector, indicating increasing career opportunities for the local population. In addition to the traditional village economy, the county has been developing tourism and secondary manufacturing as complementary sectors to its agricultural goods.

The Key Challenges

In 2018, 11,724 annual registered families in Guzhen County were classified as economically impoverished (IPRCC 2021). These families faced various barriers in escaping the poverty cycle, including limited access to quality education and healthcare services due to their low income. The key challenges identified are as follows:

1. insufficient physical and digital infrastructure
2. lengthy process in government approval procedure that affects project planning and execution
3. shortage of digital service education.

Lack of Physical and Digital Infrastructure

The lack of a physical and digital infrastructure was one of the key causes of poverty in Guzhen county. Prior to investments being made in the region, it remained a traditional village with "mud roads everywhere, which made it hard to travel to nearby cities during rainy days," (Guzhen Xian Renmin Zhengfu 2022). The inadequate transportation infrastructure in turn hindered communication between urban and rural areas. Furthermore, the absence of proper delivery stations between rural and urban regions led to higher transportation costs for villagers when exporting goods to urban areas.

The absence of a robust digital infrastructure also posed challenges in terms of information communication. Guzhen villagers had access only to conventional phones, and their internet connectivity was insufficient. This inefficient digital infrastructure made it difficult to access marketplace information such as price and quantities. This caused surpluses or shortages of goods thus failed to maximize profits.

Government Structure

One of the most prominent focal issues is the hierarchical government structure which hindered the efficiency of information transfer. The approval process from the supervising government entity caused significant time delays, resulting in severe miscommunication between government officials and villagers. This inefficiency had a particularly negative impact on the agricultural goods market, which heavily relied on real-time price and trading volume information.

Time Lag

Besides lengthy government-related procedure, the lack of information infrastructure in rural China also posed challenges to economic growth. Compared to an efficient market with quantitative demand and supply, the outdated technology and limited transparency in the market led to miscalculations in yearly production for farmers. With traditional and inadequate storage facilities, the inefficiency resulted in an imbalance between input and output, further exacerbating the challenges faced by farmers.

The Solutions

In 2018, the Agricultural Food Station app program, known as Nongliang Yizhan 农粮驿站 in Chinese, was implemented with funding of CNY 6 million by the Anhui Luxin Ecological Agriculture Co., Ltd. (安徽璐欣生态农业科技有限公司). The aim was to encourage villagers to start businesses and expand their sales network through e-commerce. Rather than a conventional business model with a single wet market in town, the farmers were introduced to various sales channels with larger market power. In addition, the program ensured both the buyers and sellers of the quality of goods sold, which indirectly increased demand and consumer confidence in the purchased meats and vegetables.

The system effectively broke down into three essential parts known as the "Agri-food stations + outlets + poverty-stricken households" poverty alleviation model ("农粮驿站 + 网点 + 贫困户" 脱贫模式). The first step was to establish the program with the support of the government. University students provided the basic program infrastructure and created an intuitive user interface for users to interact with. The second step was to create multiple outlets around rural and urban China. This establishment of outlets not only solved the problem of logistics and inefficient supply chains but also created further employment opportunities in such outlets. The third step was to use big data to match the demand for goods with farmers' supply. By matching and analyzing potential new profitable opportunities, the market size expanded along with a decrease in poverty cases.

As a direct result of the development of the Agricultural Food Station, more people were attracted to return to the county for investment opportunities. This increased the potential market size and allowed the county to transition from primary to secondary or even tertiary industry within a short period. In the long term, this would allow more talent development opportunities, ultimately helping the whole county to escape from poverty. To seek wider expansion of the market, the joint advertising of agricultural fairs and supermarkets was also necessary, as the platform required more exposure to enhance the growth rate of revenue.

The online platform with multiple functions has increased efficiency for both consumers and sellers. Consumers first place an order for the agricultural products to be purchased on the Agri-food Station app. After receiving the order, the customer service of Agricultural Food Station sorts them according to staple food, poultry, vegetables, eggs, etc. Purchasing personnel forwarded the order to the homes of poor households according to the order quantity, buy agricultural products from poor households. Then the personnel sent them to the unified designated slaughtering and processing sites in Guzhen County. Inspection, traceability and coding, packaging, packing, and delivery were carried out within the city through the courier team of poor households and delivered to consumers through courier companies in other areas. The process aligned with the that of similar sellers in urban cities, which ensures the rural economy unites with the national economy in the future. Until 2021, more than 200 types of agricultural goods were available on the platform, with a total of 36 firms. For instance, Huang Baogui is a villager who currently has more than 3,000 pigeons in a farming area of 2,000 sqm, earning over CNY 10,000 per year.

The infrastructure investment has aimed at expanding the capacity of connections. By 2022, a total of 129 roads of 61.4 km have been built. The new roads not only connected the nearby villages of Guyang, Liancheng, and Xinmaqiao to develop economic areas, but also connected major highways to major cities in Hefei and Nanjing in July 2021 (Jia 2022).

Besides physical infrastructure, a digital infrastructure such as 5G coverage has been constructed. By the end of 2020, 86 5G stations and 6,211.4 km of optic fiber network have been implemented. This allowed villagers to attain greater access to information platforms. Most of the stations were supported by 43 solar-powering batteries, reducing the power burdens during the winter.

Case Analysis

Here, we apply the PEST model (i.e., Political, Economic, Social, and Technological model) to conduct a holistic review of the case (Fig. 1).

Political Impact

The accomplishment of the project demonstrates effective coordination between the central and local governments. The process of permitting investments and infrastructure construction showcases the commitment to achieving China's new goals. This serves as a testament to the local government officials and their achievement. On a national level, the publication of these accomplishments showcases the power and capability of achieving goals. This reinforced a sense of patriotism both within and outside rural China.

Economic Impact

Once the sales channels of agricultural products opened, sales and income would increase significantly. Currently, there are over 200 kinds of agricultural products which are sold at the Agricultural Food Station. Rice, grains, black peanuts, watermelon, and other agricultural products are sold all over the country. The Agricultural Food Station now serves more than 2,200 impoverished households in the county, accounting for 19% of the county's total impoverished households. The average annual income of the poor households has increased by nearly CNY 6,000 (approximately USD 835 in 2023), an increase of 71% which contributed to stable poverty

Political	Economic
Coordination of central and local government	Increase e-commerce variety
Accomplish local government's mission	Self-sustaining economic development in long run
	Financial funding from government
Social	**Technological**
Increase standard of living in villages	Big Data and IOT tech support
Return to home village rather going into city	Equip necessary skills for long-run
Access to mainstream society	

Fig. 1 The composition of a PEST analysis

alleviation. Since the online sales price of agricultural products is generally higher than the local price, this encouraged poor households to further expand production and improve product quality. This has achieved a virtuous circle of increasing income for the poor.

Social Impact

One of the most direct impacts is the improvement in the standard of living resulting from improved telecommunications. The villagers now enjoy larger yards for growing animals and vegetables, as well as access to a wider range of consumer goods outside the village. On the other hand, urban dwellers benefit from lower prices for agricultural goods compared to before. In other words, the standard of living improves for both rural and urban residents.

An indirect outcome is the return of individuals to the village to enjoy these benefits of poverty alleviation. Rather than migrating to urban areas for work, people now have the option to pursue education outside the village and return to operate their own e-commerce business. This indirectly creates a more balanced relationship between cities and villages, providing villagers with the same opportunities as their urban counterparts.

Technological Impact

The implementation of big data not only benefits the villagers directly, but also helps researchers understand the current state of e-commerce which is existing in rural China. As rural e-commerce is integrated into the larger Chinese economy, efficient technology plays a crucial role in the process. In addition, the increase in technological support facilitates a long-run self-sustaining model, empowering farmers to take control of their own business rather than relying solely on the government assistance. The government can replicate the same technological framework in neighbouring villages, allowing the poverty alleviation project to expand to various locations.

Long-Term Impact

The Agricultural Food Station enables poor households to maintain a neutral position during market turbulence. This promotes the standardized production of agricultural products. The Agricultural Food Station provides risk protection to the farmers' produce and, at the same time, helps to accelerate the adjustment of the local agricultural industry structure. This is to produce more and better agricultural products which meet customer needs and gradually realize the scale, branding, and standardization of agricultural products.

The model has been replicated and developed in many local villages and towns. The Agricultural Food Station has been implemented on a large-scale, corporate, and market-oriented operation model. Dougou Village (陡沟村) and Liuji Town (刘集镇) started implementing the model, and town-level operation centers have been established in all towns in Guzhen County. Thirty-six agricultural and household electrical appliances stores have been opened, 18 by poor households. In the future, the Agricultural Food Station will integrate operation management, order processing, after-sales service, and AI video surveillance. A county-level data center will promote e-commerce poverty alleviation to the modern rural refined e-commerce work.

The Agricultural Food Station has accelerated the development of agricultural industry. The system also promoted the improvement of rural infrastructure such as roads, broadband networks, and electricity, as well as the year-by-year improvement of basic public services like education, medical care, and basic pensions.

Best Practice Case Reference: Social Participation in Poverty Alleviation and Development of China (中国社会扶贫网)—Poverty Alleviation Through E-Commerce

The use of e-commerce industry for poverty alleviation is not limited to Guzhen County but is implemented in other regions of China as well. In August 2020, over 5.4 million internet investment projects were accepted by the program out of 6.8 million requests, and fund exceeding CNY 115 million were raised and covering more than 280,000 villages. The core principles of the model encompass three key aspects: (a) leveraging "Internet+" to integrate offline and online systems; (b) establishing a poverty alleviation platform for quality control; and (c) utilizing big data for feedback analysis.

The Internet+ component involves matching donations of used goods and the purchase of agricultural products from poverty-stricken villages. The highly efficient information systems supporting the exchange of messages and goods benefits both parties involved, which amplified the positive impact of the donations.

The establishment of a platform focuses on bridging the supply chain gap between large firms and farmers. Through discounts and subsidies that reduced the cost of primary goods, society becomes more inclined to choose agricultural goods from villagers. This created a self-sustaining system in the long run.

Big data enabled more efficient feedback and analysis and it has ensured the smooth operation of the poverty alleviation process.

International Comparative Studies

Similar practices of poverty alleviation via e-commerce have been conducted in South Africa. In 2016, the number of SMMEs (small, micro and medium-sized enterprises) reached 2.29 million. Despite the large potential market, e-commerce is still developing because of the logistics challenges throughout the country. The South African government has introduced the Electronic Communications and Transfers (ECT) Act to regulate and promote electronic transactions by SMMEs (Mkhosi 2017).

Technologies such as big data and the Internet of Things (IoT) were developed to push e-commerce into the mainstream. Yet, the large investment required is a challenge due to the difficulty in attracting related external funds without tax relief. SMMEs also faced an inaccessible infrastructure and poor-quality telecommunications.

Key Learnings

Sustainable Development Goals

No poverty. The market for agricultural products has opened, and the market system for agricultural products has improved. This has helped to increase the income of people in Guzhen county who also alleviated their poverty. The freedom from poverty is the primary goal of sustainable development: "Eradication of Poverty in All Forms".

Quality education. The influx of talent and the development of infrastructure has created favorable conditions for improving education. In the meantime, economic growth has provided financial support for education investments. This mutually beneficial relationship between quality education and sustainable economic development reinforces and reinforces one another.

Decent jobs and economic growth. The return of residents and migration to Guzhen county have positively impacted productivity and production efficiency, leading to the promotion of full productive employment. It has supported long-term sustainable economic growth.

Industry, innovation, and infrastructure. The development of transportation and communication infrastructure not only benefited the primary industry development but also facilitated the growth of secondary and tertiary industries. Investment in infrastructure plays a crucial role in achieving sustainable development.

Other Learnings

1. The implementation of unified processing, packaging, and distribution at the agricultural and grain post station have facilitated the standardization, scalability, and branding of agricultural products.
2. It is crucial to encourage and attract new talents to contribute to the development and success of poverty alleviation initiatives.

References

Guzhen Xian Renmin Zhengfu. (2022, May 23). *Guzhen Xian Liancheng Zhen: Zhua nongcun jijian cu xiangcun zhenxing 固镇县连城镇:抓农村基建促乡村振兴* [Guzhen County Liancheng Town: Focus on rural infrastructure construction to promote rural revitalization]. Guzhen Xian Renmin Zhengfu Wang. https://www.guzhen.gov.cn/gzdt/xzzc/81244995.html

IPRCC (2021) *Global Solicitation and Challenge Prize on Best Poverty Reduction Practices 全球减贫案例征集活动* [E-Commerce Enterprise Promotes Development of the Whole Industrial Chain of Modern Agriculture – Poverty Reduction through In-Depth Integration of Agriculture and E-Commerce in Anhui's Guzhen County].

Jia, T. (2022, November 11). *Anhui Guzhen: Jianshe "si hao lu" datong "zhenxing lu" 安徽固镇:建设"四好路" 打通"振兴路"* [Guzhen Town, Anhui Province: Building "Four Good Roads" and Opening up "Road of Rejuvenation"]. Xinhua Silk Road. https://www.imsilkroad.com/news/p/496727.html

Meemi, O. (2022, January 26). A timeline of China's e-commerce sector and the evolution of Alibaba, JD, and Pinduoduo. *Investor Insights Asia*. https://www.investorinsights.asia/post/understanding-the-evolution-of-china-s-e-commerce-empire

Mkhosi, P. (2017). *National report on e-commerce development in South Africa* (Inclusive and Sustainable Industrial Development Working Paper Series WP 18). United Nations Industrial Development Organization. https://www.unido.org/sites/default/files/2017-10/WP_18_2017.pdf

Yuanlong Village Eco-migration

Humanity is to maintain harmony with Mother Nature, and
"the relationship between the two is one of symbiosis."
(Xi, 2017)

This case study delves into the concept of eco-migration, a central component of China's 12th Five-Year Plan and a top priority for the Chinese Communist Party (CCP). According to XI Jinping's words, eco-migration addresses the pressing issue of human beings' relationship with their natural environment. The successful pilot experiment of eco-migration in Yuanlong village (原隆村) serves as the focal point of this study. It highlights the factors that contributed to Yuanlong's success, with particular emphasis on the collaboration between provinces. The subsequent improvements in industrial structure and the significant role of the CCP as the project initiator in poverty alleviation efforts will also be discussed. Ultimately, the last section describes Yuanlong as a model of global recognition.

Background

The focal village, Yuanlong, which is located in Minning Town under the administration of Yongning County, Ningxia Hui Autonomous Region, has been well-known for its remarkable achievements in poverty alleviation through eco-migration since 2019 when the village shook off its poverty hat. Yuanlong quickly became the largest eco-migration village in Minning Town under the CCP's 12th (i.e., 2011–2015) Five-Year Plan. Further recognition came from a red-themed Chinese TV series titled *Minning Town* in 2021, which brought the village's story to countless households. The Yuanlong eco-relocation project was carried out with the collaborative efforts involving

International Poverty Reduction Center In China, *Poverty Alleviation Case Analysis In China*, SpringerBriefs on Case Studies of Sustainable Development,
https://doi.org/10.1007/978-981-97-4537-1_11

the local government, enterprises, and individual villagers, driven by the CCP slogan "Community of Common Destiny from Poverty Towards Prosperity" with a specific focus on eco-migration.

Eco-migration

Challenges

The motivation behind the transformation and the initial catalyst for change in Yuanlong are worth examining. "Yuanlong" was established and named after the transformation, as it was *not* the village's original name. It originated as Xihaigu (西海固), the former hometown of Yuanlong villagers, which is situated in the mountainous region of southern Ningxia Hui Autonomous Region. In 1972, the United Nations Food and Agriculture Development Agency classified Xihaigu as one of the least suitable areas for human settlement and survival. An interviewee who had previously lived in Xihaigu inhabitant and now resides in Yuanlong expressed that after 40 years in Xihaigu, there were hardly any cherished memories. His sole focus was survival (Guojia Fazhan Gaige Wei 2020). The area was characterized by extreme poverty, marked by scarcity of clean water, green mountain ranges, and a history marred by land reclamation, drought, desertification, steep and barren land, mud caves, and a fragile ecological environment (Anonymous 2021). The phrase which best described the situation is "absolute poverty."

Water scarcity posed a severe challenge, making it difficult for the inhabitants to meet their basic needs and generate household income. Prior to relocation, the indigenous population struggled to attain stability and a basic income due to natural disasters and inadequate supportive policies (Zhao et al. 2021).

At the individual level, in a societal group where there were hardly any educational resources, literacy among all age groups was far from satisfactory. To "address the people's most immediate concerns" was prioritized in the CCP's agenda to improve the well-being of citizens. The party also emphasized the concept and mission of "harmonious coexistence between humans and the natural environment," with "the prosperity of human civilization hinging on a prosperous ecosystem." To ensure this, a large-scale relocation project was initiated. China had long been plagued by poverty issues, the scale and severity of which were huge and rarely observed in other parts of the globe (State Council 2021). These poverty-stricken areas have a history of inadequate infrastructure, limited public services, and overall economic underdevelopment.

Actions Speak Louder Than Words

Around 1982 to 1983, Stage 1, "Diao Zhuang Migration" (吊庄移民), i.e., to relocate citizens from an ecologically fragile environment to uncultivated lands suitable for living commenced with the goal of ending regional environmental damage in three years and diminishing hunger in five years. The emphasis in Stage 1 was to improve citizens' well-being, such as reducing poverty and achieving food safety rather than to make dramatic changes to the environment.

After the initial stage, the emphasis then shifted in 2001 to improving the ecosystem with the publication of "Implementation Advice on Poverty Alleviation Relocation Pilot Projects" by the State Development Planning Commission. The focus of Stage 2 was not only to reduce poverty but also to recover and ameliorate the situation in the new territories (Ding 2015). The connection between human beings and the environment was enhanced.

Still, circumstances did not improve in just a few years. In 2013, Yuanlong was confirmed as one of the major, severely impoverished villages. The poverty incidence was 38.98% with 3,747 impoverished villagers from 776 families identified in the following year (Briefing n.d.).

Remaining Problems and Approaches

To assess the quality of life for Yuanlong citizens, Chinese scholars have identified six key factors: (a) basic infrastructure, (b) economic income growth, (c) neighbourhood relationships, (d) governmental policies, (e) the lifestyle of ethnic minority groups, and (f) community environment. These factors were ranked based on their impact, with basic infrastructure being the most influential (a detailed elaboration in Chinese can be viewed in Zhao et al. 2022). However, problems were identified in each of these areas.

One significant challenge arose from clashes between different ethnic groups. The origin and ancestors of Yuanlong villagers are mainly Han ethnic group from Longde County (35.3%) and Hui minority (sometimes referred to by scholars as Chinese Muslims) from Yuanzhou District (64.7%) in the city of Guyuan (Du 2017). These two groups had limited exposure to each other's cultures (Wu 2016). To address these clashes, the CCP's branch in Yuanlong initiated regular meetings and social activities between the two groups to promote camaraderie. Efforts were also made to establish different dispute-resolution mechanisms (Wu 2016). In 2014, out of the 900 citizens dispute settlements at village-level public agencies, 600 cases were successfully handled immediately, and the remaining 300 were resolved through collaboration between the village and town levels (Wu 2016).

Another challenging aspect was the reluctance of older generations to leave their ancestral homes and the roots of their family tree, despite the willingness of younger generations to relocate. This created disagreements between citizens and the public sector during the relocation process. Faced with funding issues and pressure from citizens and the party state, the government employed various carrot-and-stick approaches. This included expounding on the benefits of relocation for future generations and offering subsidies and rewards to those who agreed to migrate. In some cases, it did some arm-twisting. The public had high expectations of the government performance about the relocation, putting pressure on the local government to produce better results.

Green Development in Education

Education as a task was also on the agenda of Yuanlong, especially regarding citizens' environmental awareness. The CCP recognized the importance of developing a sense of global citizenship and self-identity among the villagers. To achieve this, the government organized internal competitions among family units, where households were evaluated based on their contributions and efforts in community and environmental services. These initiatives were in line with guidelines outlined in the regulatory document titled "Opinions of the State Council Leading Group Office of Poverty Alleviation and Development on Jointly Promoting the Work of Whole-Village Advancement, Poverty Alleviation and Development," which states that:

> The spiritual civilization development steering department shall take the improvement of peasants' civilization quality as the objective, take the creation of civilized villages and townships as the carrier, take the ideas and beliefs education, the establishment of civilization and new ethos, the rectification of dirty and disordered environments and the building of a service system as key tasks, and focus on the cultivation of new peasants, advocacy of new practice, creation of a new environment, construction of a new culture, so as to further strengthen the building of spiritual civilization in rural areas. The spiritual civilization development steering department shall further carry out the activities of creating civilized ecological villages, star civilized households, civilized creditworthy households and civilized small townships.

The sense of responsibility and dedication to the environment is now deep-rooted in every Yuanlong villager, while the biggest beneficiary is nature. According to Yuanlong Secretary of the Party Committee, 598 households received the recognition as highly commended and 20 households as civilized, highlighting their exemplary contributions to environmental protection. Additonally, CNY 235,500 were distributed to citizens through the environmental protection point redemption scheme over several months.

Before the relocation, the uncultivated lands had a weak foundation for environmental sustainability. The lack of expertise in agriculture and sustainable industries among government officials and migration initiators posed a challenge (Jiang et al. 2010). Recognizing this need, collaboration between provinces played a crucial role in addressing these challenges.

Collaboration Between Two Provinces

The collaboration between two provinces, Fujian province and Ningxia Hui autonomous region, played a crucial role in addressing the challenges faced in Yuanlong and promoting green development in education. The concept of collaboration between eastern and western provinces was initiated by the State Council in September 1996 as a major poverty alleviation model. Under this plan, 13 eastern provinces were paired with 10 western provinces to provide support and assistance.

Fujian, a coastal province in southeastern China, was paired with Ningxia, where Yuanlong village is located, despite the significant distance of more than a thousand miles between them. In November 1996, a specialist group led by Xi Jinping, who was the Deputy Secretary of the Fujian provincial Party Committee at that time, was formed to facilitate the collaboration. Xi later named the town Minning, combining "Min" from Fujian and "Ning" from Ningxia.

The first collaborative project carried out by the East (Min)—est (Ning) Model was the aforementioned Stage 1 Diao Zhuang Migration. The two provinces inaugurated Minning village on the Diao Zhuang Migration spot, with its current name Minning Town.

Over 20 years, Ningxia received massive support from Fujian province in terms of finance and human resources. Donated money from the Fujian government reached more than CNY 1.28 billion (People.cn 2016). Fujian sent 11 teams of 183 public servants, plus 2,000 experts of different professions to assist Ningxia. Moreover, Fujian provided jobs for over 50,000 impoverished people from Ningxia (Zhang 2021).

But it was clear to the state-level administration that if Fujian's role in Ningxia was just for financial support, the whole effort would be a one-way donation, which hardly provided any incentives for Fujian in the long run. Therefore, the government came up with an even bigger strategy of turning the donation into a sustainable give-and-take model that highlighted mutual concessions and reciprocity. It did this mainly by launching Fujian industries in Yuanlong. In 1997, the first industry with Yuanlong-specific characteristics, *juncao* (菌草) technology, i.e., a technology consists of the cultivation of a grass that can be used as a substrate for mushroom production, feed for animals, windbreaks, and to minimize soil erosion, was established with the assistance of the Fujian province. This attracted investment from Fujian enterprises. The application of Juncao technology in Yuanlong, which was developed by the National Engineering Research Center for Juncao Technology of the Fujian Agriculture and Forestry University of China, signified a future for sustainable agricultural development (Anonymous 2022a). It could be used to cultivate medicinal mushrooms or simply to feed livestock or hinder soil erosion, which stops desertification (Anonymous 2022a). The East–West cooperation between the two provinces also occurred in the wine industry.

The two provinces have continued their long-lasting collaboration. The 26th Joint Meeting of Min-Ning-Cooperation was held on 4 September 2022 (Anonymous 2022b), the latest meeting minutes signed by the two governments. It planned to further enhance the collaboration in industries, employments, talents, education, technology, health care, consumption, etc. In terms of industrial partnerships, various models of Fujian businesses with Ningxia resources, Ningxia businesses with Fujian resources, Fujian headquarters with Ningxia offices, Ningxia headquarters with Fujian offices, Fujian markets with Ningxia products, Ningxia markets with Fujian products were fostered. The two also explored potential linkups in the use of big data (Anonymous 2022b). The joint meeting was another big step forward from the 25th Joint Meeting held in 2022, at which financial support funds from Fujian reached CNY 610 million, 250 Fujian-Ningxia projects were initiated and implemented, and 166 new companies were to invest locally with actual paid-in capital of CNY 3.15 billion. The numbers are still rising.

Case Analysis: Multidimensional Industries

Agriculture

Many land relocation and circulation projects were designed and carried out, which led to related industrial adjustments in crops and livestock production structures. The aggregate total land circulation was estimated at 421 hectares. Yuanlong witnessed the prosperity of the wine and raspberry industries when some Fujian merchants moved to the village to develop their businesses. In the meantime, it created tens of thousands of job opportunities for local villagers. The wine and raspberry industries were two giant agriculture sectors in Yuanlong. Subsequently, several farming enterprises were introduced to set up their factories in the village. A complete value chain with Yuanlong characteristics of a green development theme which includes livestock production, cultivation, and wholesaling has been reinforced.

Labor Supply and Commerce

The typical form of labor chain supply in Yuanlong is geographical proximity with the main source of labor is immigrants from nearby villages. The work requirement has developed from farming and livestock production to more modern manufacturing and e-commerce industry.

Yuanlong's special e-commerce platforms have advanced to the stage of an e-commerce industry. The local and Fujian provincial governments and corporations further developed Yuanlong's reputation as a modern e-commerce village. The village used online shopping platforms to establish marketing strategies. The products Yuanlong sells online are typically connected to the theme of green development, for which the village has been known. Among villagers who devote their time and effort to the e-commerce industry, those with extraordinary sales skills were given special titles so they are recognized by online customers nationwide to promote Yuanlong-made products.

Other Industries

The photovoltaic industry, also considered as one of the leading industries in Yuanlong, has tight connection with the village's green development blueprint. Again, the prosperity of the photovoltaic industry started with four giant companies which had relatively more financial resources and expertise. They analyzed Yuanlong's special geographic location and invested in huge research projects to utilize solar radiation as the original raw source of electricity. Shareholders of the businesses included Yuanlong itself and its villagers, who became, through an arrangement, the beneficiaries.

Tourism also developed inYuanlong, with its close desert mountain range which was a famous attraction. Successful tourism created numerous job opportunities and enhanced green development. Therefore, the notion of green development and the success of Yuanlong stemmed from the substantial development of multidimensional industries.

CCP's Directions

The massive project's success spanning several decades is due to multiple contributing factors, mainly the collaboration between the two provinces, citizens themselves, and the general guidance offered by the government.

Key CCP officials paid special attention to the development of Yuanlong since they considered it a pilot project on poverty reduction and rural revitalization through eco-emigration. In order to boost internal efficiency, the government sent clear proposals and slogans to detail the steps and work required on the administrative level. The authorities defined the general plan for the village as a "political agenda" to conduct to the full extent. The government only emphasized the importance of catering to the citizens' basic needs by setting the principle of "to supply what is demanded instantly" and at the same time endeavored to tailor policies for each household. The government further established 13 online official party groups to improve villagers' quality of life, including education, recreation, medical health care, career development, and so forth. The utility of its official administration was maximized in order to foster Yuanlong's successful transformation.

Serving the Globe

The No poverty goal of the UN's SDG is to "eradicate extreme poverty for all people everywhere in all its forms" by 2030. At the time the current study was written, only seven years remain. China is now 10 years ahead of the UN schedule in terms of complete eradication of extreme poverty (State Council 2021). The country deserves praise for its contribution to humankind. Despite Yuanlong's relatively young history of 10 years, the pre-renovation preparation work went on for more than two decades. To put forward with such a massive plan requires time and commitment. The case of Yuanlong might be a great example to the world, if governments and organizations worldwide apply the same or similar method to other rural areas in desperate need of eco-migration to alleviate poverty.

From a practical standpoint, a poverty alleviation project or any population movement aimed at reducing poverty similar to Yuanlong, must be accompanied by appropriate public policy interventions. In recent years, climate change has induced extensive environmental degradation, leading to migration becoming a prevalent solution for many affected populations. However, addressing these challenges is beyond the capabilities of less developed countries alone, due to factors such as differing political systems, financial constraints, responses from the affected citizens, and the risk of potential human rights violations. Migration often gives rise to vaious forms of conflict, including sociological, psychological, economic, and political tensions. Nonetheless, public policy can play a role in facilitating eco-migration (Reuveny 2008), as exemplified by the case of Yuanlong, further reinforcing this assertion.

The response of governments and private sectors to eco-migration issues largely depend on their own awareness of the topic, its severity, and its profound meaning for the underprivileged. The case of Yuanlong, particularly its profound impact on both humankind and nature, can also serve as an ESG indicator. While the Yuanlong project possibly achieved significant poverty reduction, the initiators of the project have always been mindful of environmental protection. As a result, improvements in safeguarding the environment have come along with the poverty reduction efforts. The popularity of green bond principles bears some similarities to the current case, as the public has embraced the concept of using financial leverage to address nonfinancial issues. When ESG finance advances towards sustainable development, poverty reduction can also be an effective approach to achieving sustainable environment. Since COVID-19, eco-friendliness and social responsibility have become central policies for governments worldwide, evident from the additional sections on government and parliamentary webpages. This case study of Yuanlong as a parable for green development aims to serve the global community in addressing environmental issues while simultaneously reducing poverty.

Best Practice: Poverty alleviation by relocating the poor (with industry creation and financial aid) at Hubei

Hubei Province had large amount of relocation projects (10% of the whole country) to be carried out, which means that large amount of resources, planning and coordination was required. A coordinated system had been introduced to manage fund-raising, strategic planning, governance and management of the finance and human resource. One of the good examples is Hubei Poverty Alleviation investment and development Limited Company.

Innovation in governance has been in place which connects resources efficiently to strategic planning of new industry development and the need of the people.

For the funds for specific poverty alleviation project use, a full-chain contract system and operation mechanism of "investment, control and repayment" has been established. Each special fund allocation has a set of strict standard procedures. When the funds are invested, the project scale and capital needs had to be carefully assessed. The qualifications of the project-leading company, the fund release and repayment requirements would also be strictly reviewed, while a fund supervision agreement was to be signed.

The use of each special fund has a complete and full-coverage supervision mechanism, including the implementation of dynamic tracking of the leading business entity, the establishment of a complete ledger system for the data collection and analysis, spot-checks and inspections of the project fund use management, and real-time supervision of the cash flow of special funds.

With the coordinated efforts, RMB 10 billion had been allocated to 57 relocation projects in 2016. Each project was followed by a well-planned governance system to monitor the progress and status of all related aspects.

Hubei Poverty Alleviation Investment Group had supported the "Mushroom Town" with the construction funds for housing and supporting infrastructure, public service facilities, industry park supporting facilities. They had achieved poverty alleviation via industry creation. While leading the social asset management, they have established a new model "Leading enterprise + Cooperative + Industry base + farmer" for targeted poverty alleviation.

The relocated families could feel the sense of belonging, stability, identity-recognition and happiness.

References

Anonymous. (2021, November 16). Xi Focus-closeup: Xi's four trips to China's "most uninhabitable place". *Xinhua Net*. http://www.news.cn/english/2021-11/16/c_1310314796.htm

Anonymous. (2022a, March 11). Feature: Chinese Juncao technology spells bright future for Tanzania's mushroom growers. *Xinhua Net*. https://english.news.cn/20220311/4ec0024441dc491b9de48bdba66797fd/c.html

Anonymous. (2022b, September 4). Duo lingyu shenhua hezuo zhutui Minning xiezuo shengji 多领域深化合作助推闽宁协作升级 [Deepening cooperation in multiple fields promotes the upgrading of Minning cooperation]. *Xinhua Net*. http://www.news.cn/local/2022-09/04/c_1128975159.htm

Briefing. (n.d.). Ningxia Yongning Xian Minning Zhen Yuanlong Xun 宁夏永宁县闽宁镇原隆村 [Yuanlong Village, Minning Town, Yongning County, Ningxia]. In *Quanguo tuopin gongjian jiaoliu jidi jianjie (shang ce) 全国脱贫攻坚交流基地简介(上册)* [Introduction to the National Exchange Base for Poverty Alleviation (Volume 1)] (pp. 141–144).

Ding, S. (2015). *The ecological migration study in the Ningxiu Province: A case on the M Town* [Dotoral dissertation, Lanzhou University]. CNKI. https://kns.cnki.net/KCMS/detail/detail.aspx?dbname=CDFDLAST2017&filename=1015352426.nh

Du, S. (2017). "Minning moshi" shuxie dong xi chanye fupin xiezuo xin fanben "闽宁模式"书写东西产业扶贫协作新范本 ["Minning Model" creates a new model of poverty alleviation cooperation between eastern and western region industries in China]. *Xin Xibu*, (11), 21–24. http://industry.wanfangdata.com.cn/dl/Detail/Periodical?id=Periodical_xxb201711015

Guojia Fazhan Gaige Wei. (2020, October 27). Ci xin an chu shi wu xiang: Ningxia fupin yimin banqian gongzuo chengjiu yu jingyan zongshu 此心安处是吾乡——宁夏扶贫移民搬迁工作成就与经验综述 ["Home" is where one's heart settles in: A summary of the achievements and experiences of Ningxia poverty alleviation and immigrant relocation work] [Platform]. https://bit.ly/ningxias-poverty-alleviation-and-immigrant-relocation-work

Jiang, Y., Su, H., Huang, S., & Lin, Z. (2010). Ningxia shengtai yimin diqu nongcun ganqun guanxi de diaocha fenxi: Yi Minning Zhen wei li 宁夏生态移民地区农村干群关系的调查分析——以闽宁镇为例 [Investigation and analysis of the relationship between rural cadres and the masses in the ecological immigration area of Ningxia: Taking Minning Town as an example]. *Neimenggu Keji Yu Jingji*, (06), 39–40 & 44. https://mqikan.cqvip.com/Article/ArticleDetail?id=33570335&from=Article_Index

Reuveny, R. (2008). Ecomigration and violent conflict: Case studies and public policy implications. *Human Ecology*, *36*(1), 1–13. https://doi.org/10.1007/s10745-007-9142-5

State Council. (2021, April 6). *White paper: Poverty alleviation: China's experience and contribution* [White paper]. The State Council Information Office of the People's Republic of China. http://www.china.org.cn/chinese/2021-06/02/content_77513397.htm

Wu, C. (2016). Yuanong Cun: Yimin xincun de meili tuibian fankai Minning Zhen jianshe fazhan xin pianzhang xilie baodao zhi er 原隆村:移民新村的美丽蜕变——翻开闽宁镇建设发展新篇章系列报道之二 [Yuanlong Village: The beautiful transformation of the new immigrant village—Opening a new chapter in the construction and development of Minning Town, Part 2]. In Yongning Xian Shizhi Bianzuan Weiyuanhui Bangongshi 永宁县史志编纂委员会办公室 (Ed.), *2016 Yongnig Nianjian 2016 永宁年鉴* (pp. 362–363). Ningxia People's Publishing House.

Xi, J. (2017, October 27). Juesheng quanmian jiancheng xiaokang shehui, duoqu xinshidai Zhongguo tese shehui zhuyi weida shengli: Zai Zhongguo Gongchandang di shijiu ci quanguo daibiao dahui shang de baogao 决胜全面建成小康社会 夺取新时代中国特色社会主义伟大胜利——在中国共产党第十九次全国代表大会上的报告 [Decisive victory in building a well-off society in an all-round way, and winning the great victory of socialism with Chinese characteristics in the new era: Report at the 19th National Congress of the Communist Party of China]. *Xinhua Net*. http://www.xinhuanet.com//politics/19cpcnc/2017-10/27/c_1121867529.htm

Zhang, Z. (2021, April 18). *Pooling strengths for poverty alleviation works miracle.* Embassy of the People's Republic of China in the Republic of North Macedonia. http://mk.china-embassy.gov.cn/eng/brns/202104/t20210419_8957951.htm

Zhao, D., Cao, J., & Tian, W. (2021). Shengtai yimin shequ shenghuo kongjian yanhua ji zhiliang pingjia: Yi Ningxia Yinchuan Shi Minning Zhen weili 生态移民社区生活空间之演化及质量评价——以宁夏银川市闽宁镇为例 [Evolution and quality evaluation of living space in ecological migration community: Taking Minning Town as an example]. *Ningxia Shehui Kexue,* (6), 180–188. https://lxsk.cbpt.cnki.net/WKB/WebPublication/paperDigest.aspx?paperID=748e0050-835f-4eef-b9fc-621c2c8002e1

GPSR Compliance

The European Union's (EU) General Product Safety Regulation (GPSR) is a set of rules that requires consumer products to be safe and our obligations to ensure this.

If you have any concerns about our products, you can contact us on ProductSafety@springernature.com

In case Publisher is established outside the EU, the EU authorized representative is:

Springer Nature Customer Service Center GmbH
Europaplatz 3
69115 Heidelberg, Germany

The manufacturer's authorised representative in the EU is Springer Nature Customer Service Centre GmbH, Europaplatz 3, 69115 Heidelberg, Germany. If you have any concerns regarding our products, please contact ProductSafety@springernature.com

Printed and bound by CPI Group (UK) Ltd, Croydon, CR0 4YY
01/10/2026
02225880-0015